THE BOMB

THE BOMB

A PARTIAL HISTORY

OBERON BOOKS
LONDON

WWW.OBERONBOOKS.COM

This collection first published in 2012 by Oberon Books Ltd
521 Caledonian Road, London N7 9RH
Tel: +44 (0) 20 7607 3637 / Fax: +44 (0) 20 7607 3629
e-mail: info@oberonbooks.com
www.oberonbooks.com

A catalogue record for this book is available from the British
Library.

ISBN: 978-1-84943-152-1

Cover image: Atomic Blast; US marines watch the mushroom
cloud from an atomic explosion rise above the Yucca flats,
Nevada during a US nuclear weapons test. 08 May 1945.
(Photo by Keystone/Getty Images)

Printed and bound by CPI Group (UK) Ltd, Croydon, CR0 4YY.

CONTENTS

INTRODUCTION

Two years ago Baroness Shirley Williams (then Adviser on Nuclear Proliferation to Prime Minister Gordon Brown) asked my why, as the final decision date for the Trident renewal programme was approaching, the theatre was not tackling the nuclear weapons debate. These plays were conceived out of that conversation and challenge.

As I thought about how to treat this subject I realised that my whole life had been lived in the shadow of the nuclear bomb. I was born in the year the atom bomb was dropped on Hiroshima and Nagasaki, I was at school during the Cuban Missile Crisis when the real possibility of nuclear war affected us each day, I became politically aware during the heyday of CND, I lived through the worries of fall-out from atmospheric testing, and now hear the almost daily news bulletins about the nuclear threat from Iran, North Korea or from rogue terrorist groups. For these reasons it became clear that the simplest way to treat this subject would be to focus on the political landmarks involving the threat or development of nuclear weapons.

However with the commissioning of the nine writers the project evolved, and took on a life of its own. Instead of a series of plays looking at the major events such as the decision to drop the bomb on Japan, the Cuban Missile Crisis or the negotiations in Reykjavík, we decided to focus on 'Proliferation' in the first part: the decision to acquire the bomb or, more hopefully, to disarm. And in the second part to focus on the 'Present Dangers' we face in the Middle East, North Korea, and persisting with our own 'independent' nuclear deterrent. We will also be adding some verbatim voices from the military, politics and academia (edited by Richard Norton-Taylor), which extend the discussion to examine some of the nuclear choices facing the world today.

The two parts are very much, in all senses of the word, a 'partial' history of the bomb. It just was not possible to address all aspects of such a huge subject. However, I hope that these plays will cover many aspects of the nuclear debate, and be both an exciting and challenging experience for the audience. Most of all, I hope they will raise awareness of the issues, as well as stimulating and entertaining you.

Nicolas Kent
Artistic Director

THE TRICYCLE THEATRE

'Under the doughty directorship of Nicolas Kent, the
Tricycle has established itself as the foremost political
theatre in Britain, with a succession of illuminating, notably
even-handed documentary dramas on subjects ranging from
the death of Stephen Lawrence to last summer's riots.'
Charles Spencer, *The Daily Telegraph* (December 2011)

The Tricycle is proud to be working in the London borough of
Brent. During the last 30 years, the Tricycle has enjoyed a unique
reputation for high artistic achievement and inclusive education and
community work. Open all day, seven days a week, the Tricycle not
only houses a 235-seat theatre, a 300-seat cinema, gallery, bar and
cafe, but also a painting studio for young people, a rehearsal room
and the Creative Space, dedicated to working with children and
young people at risk of social exclusion. Its Education Department
provides workshops, youth theatres and special performances for
46,000 children and young people annually.

'An inspirational example of how art with a social
conscience need not require creative compromise'
Liberty Human Rights Award, 2010

The Tricycle presents an eclectic, multi-cultural programme
– in particular plays by black, Irish, Jewish, Asian and South
African writers, as well as responding to contemporary issues
and events with its ground-breaking 'tribunal plays' and
political work. In 1994, it staged the first of its 'tribunal plays':
Half the Picture by Richard Norton-Taylor and John McGrath
(a dramatisation of the Scott arms-to-Iraq inquiry), which was
the first play ever to be performed in the Houses of Parliament.
The next, marking the 50th anniversary of the 1946 war crimes
tribunal, was *Nuremberg*, which was followed by *Srebrenica* –
the 1996 UN Rule 61 hearings, which later transferred to the
National Theatre and the Belfast Festival. In 1999, the Tricycle's
reconstruction of the Stephen Lawrence inquiry, *The Colour of Justice*,

transferred to the West End and the National Theatre. In 2003, *Justifying War – Scenes from the Hutton Inquiry* opened at the Tricycle. *Bloody Sunday – Scenes from the Saville Inquiry* followed in 2005 and was also performed at the Abbey in Dublin, Belfast and Derry – it received an Olivier Award for Outstanding Achievement. *Called to Account: The Indictment of Anthony Charles Lynton Blair for the Crime of Aggression Against Iraq – A Hearing* was staged at the Tricycle with evidence from Richard Perle, the Chilean Ambassador to the UN, and ex-cabinet minister Clare Short. All of these plays have been broadcast by the BBC on radio or television, and have together reached audiences of over 34 million people worldwide.

'Offers the most politically audacious programming of any theatre in London'
Financial Times, 2010

In 2004, *Guantanamo: Honor Bound to Defend Freedom* transferred to the New Ambassadors Theatre in the West End and to the Culture Project in New York. It also played in the Houses of Parliament and on Capitol Hill in Washington, DC. It has since been performed around the world and in the USA through the Guantanamo Reading Project, which develops community productions of readings of the play – 32 performances have already been held in cities across America.

In 2006, the Tricycle received the Evening Standard Special Award for its pioneering work in political theatre.

West End transfers from the Tricycle include *The Amen Corner* by James Baldwin, the Fats Waller musical *Ain't Misbehavin'*, *Guantanamo* and *The Price* by Arthur Miller. Transfers to Broadway include the South African musical *Kat and the Kings* (two 1999 Olivier Awards for Best New Musical and Best Actor – awarded to the entire cast), as well as *Stones in His Pockets* by Marie Jones and *The 39 Steps* adapted by Patrick Barlow (both of which won Olivier Awards in the West End for Best New Comedy).

'Britain's leading political playhouse'
The Times, 2011 (leading article)

In the summer of 2009, the Tricycle launched its seven-hour trilogy about Afghanistan, *The Great Game*, which was later nominated for an Olivier Award for Outstanding Achievement. The production returned to the Tricycle in the autumn of 2010 before embarking on a tour of the USA, starting in Washington, then travelling to Minneapolis, Berkeley and New York. In February 2011, the production played two command performances for Pentagon staff, the military, policy-makers and guests in Washington. In 2010, the Tricycle won the Liberty Human Rights Arts Award.

In 2011, The Tricycle presented the World Premiere of *Tactical Questioning: Scenes from the Baha Mousa Inquiry*, edited by Richard Norton-Taylor and directed by Nicolas Kent. In the months following the London riots, the Tricycle mounted its own investigation into the summer's unrest and produced its latest verbatim play *The Riots*, which opened to critical acclaim in November 2011 and transferred to the Bernie Grant Arts Centre in Tottenham. The Tricycle also transferred its production of *Broken Glass*, starring Antony Sher and Tara FitzGerald, from the Tricycle Theatre to the Vaudeville Theatre in the West End.

**'Nicolas Kent, who has made the Tricycle
the most newsworthy theatre in London,
directs his farewell production.'**

Michael Billington, *The Guardian*, 30 Dec 2011

CREATIVE TEAM

Director	Nicolas Kent
Designer	Polly Sullivan
Video Designer	Douglas O'Connell
Lighting Designer	Howard Harrison
Sound Designer	Tom Lishman
Assistant Director	Tara Robinson
Associate Lighting Designers	Jack Knowles/Charlie Hayday
Associate Costume Designer	Sydney Florence
Associate Producer	Zoë Ingenhaag
Dramaturg	Jack Bradley
Casting Directors	Suzanne Crowley and Gilly Poole
Verbatim edited by	Richard Norton-Taylor
Production Manager	Shaz McGee
Company Stage Manager	Lizzie Chapman
Deputy Stage Manager	Charlotte Padgham
Assistant Stage Managers	Julia Blom and Helen Stone
Wardrobe Mistress	Anna Bliss Scully
Costume Assistants	Megan Cassidy
	Elizabeth Harkin
	Daisy Marcuzzi
	Hannah Mason
	Johanna Pan
	Hannah Spearing
Wigs	John Lee
Facial Hair Creation	Leanne Lashbrook
Press Representative	Emma Holland
Dialect Coach	Majella Hurley
Production Electrician	Charlie Hayday
Chief Electrician *(First Blast)*	Andy Furby
Chief Electrician *(Second Blast)*	Hadyn Williams

Tricycle crew
Leo Flint, Aidan Lesser, Paul Kizintas, Ben Jones, Elz,
Alex Melkis and Dario Fusco.

Set built by Russell Carr (russcarr@googlemail.com)
Andy Stubbs Scenic Productions

Special thanks to

FIRST BLAST: PROLIFERATION

FROM ELSEWHERE: THE MESSAGE...
by Zinnie Harris

First production
The Tricycle Theatre, London, 9th February 2012

Characters / Cast

RUDOLF	Rick Warden
OTTO	Daniel Rabin
CLERK	Simon Chandler
Director	*Nicolas Kent*

FROM ELSEWHERE: THE MESSAGE...

Two men stand in an ornate hallway on the way in to Whitehall.

The year is 1940.

The men are slightly scruffy, the setting is ornate.

RUDOLF: schön
   lieblich
   verwunderungsaufschrei

OTTO: in English! Rudolf please.

   Beat.

RUDOLF: OK. In English.
   wow.

   They look around again.

OTTO: what were you expecting?

RUDOLF: I don't know
   not this
   not something so...?

OTTO: ornate?

RUDOLF: British
   quintessentially British
   we should have worn suits

OTTO: sandbags are everywhere, don't worry about it
   tape is over the windows look

RUDOLF: OK, but ironed our shirts

OTTO: I did iron my shirt
   and I polished my shoes

RUDOLF: did you?

OTTO: yes

RUDOLF: what with?

OTTO looks at his shoes.

They don't look that great.

OTTO: we're scientists, they will understand.
we spend our lives in a laboratory
underground mainly
anyway we have some information that is all.
information about a miscalculation
it shouldn't matter if we came in our undergarments

Beat.

OTTO: your hand is shaking

RUDOLF: is it?

OTTO: you know it is

RUDOLF: I'm sorry I am not as calm as you

OTTO: I didn't say I was calm

RUDOLF: could be all this, this sense of –
do you think the paintings are to make you nervous?

OTTO: no

RUDOLF: thousands of eyes looking at you
judging you
even if there are sandbags and the dust is thick three inches
they still –
what are you doing here?
you are not British
you weren't born here were you?
good God man, you speak English even with a German
accent
you're through and through German in fact
you're one of the hun!
your name is Rudolf for god's sake

you were born in Berlin
and you're jewish, which is better only marginally
you are expecting the great British government to trust
you?

OTTO: we are a messenger that is all.

RUDOLF: look at that one, an admiral from centuries gone by

OTTO: Nelson

RUDOLF: you can never be as British as me he is saying

OTTO: yes, I was born in Austria I admit
but I live in Birmingham *now*
I work in Birmingham *now*
I like Birmingham *now*
surprisingly
we've applied for British citizenship and if it hadn't taken
so long to get it to these dusty corridors –
and anyway look to our actions, when we found the
miscalculation
we could have sat back
couldn't we, hmm?
done nothing
'how fascinating' we could have said
'Bohr got it wrong'
'how interesting'
'how theoretically interesting'
and that could have been it
finished
but we didn't do that.
we picked up the telephone. We told someone.
British
we knew we had to tell someone.
British

RUDOLF: and what if we are wrong?

Bohr was right?

OTTO: you know we aren't wrong
we spent seven days checking the mathematics
you might wish we were wrong, but you know we aren't.

Beat.

OTTO: your hand still is shaking

RUDOLF: it has a life of its own

OTTO: put it in your pocket then

RUDOLF: my glasses have broken

OTTO: what?

RUDOLF: I was going to get them out, just now to look at the
paintings, but

He takes them out.

They're smashed.

OTTO: when did they break?

RUDOLF: I wasn't observing them

OTTO: on the train?

RUDOLF: Yes I suppose

OTTO: has it ever happened before?

RUDOLF: no

OTTO: so just today?

RUDOLF: yes

OTTO: the day we go to Whitehall
can you see without them?

RUDOLF: of course I can
see something

OTTO: so it is OK then

RUDOLF: a blob and a shape
but the detail, no

OTTO: Good grief Rudolf

RUDOLF puts the glasses on.

OTTO: you can't wear them

RUDOLF: you said we were only messengers, it doesn't matter
what we look like

OTTO: take them off

RUDOLF: you'll have to go through the calculations then

OTTO: it's in your writing

RUDOLF: you can read it

OTTO: du drecksack, you don't have spare glasses?

RUDOLF: why would I carry spare glasses?

OTTO: in case this happens

RUDOLF: this wasn't predictable
this wasn't something that in the grand scheme of things
was very likely

OTTO: nothing is predictable, you cover yourself for all
outcomes

RUDOLF: did you bring a spare pair of trousers in case you sat
in some shit?

Beat.

OTTO: do you know the mathematics off by heart?

RUDOLF: yes

OTTO: you'll have to recite it then.

RUDOLF: it would take a week

OTTO: let's hope they are typical politicians
only interested in the message

RUDOLF: when it is as important as this

OTTO: they'll get their own physicists to work on it
they'll ring up Oliphant and the rest
the best British brains

RUDOLF: no, they'll cross-question and double-check every
single of our assumptions, every prediction, every thought
about a prediction
I can't go in there without wearing my glasses it's
impossible
I'm sorry

OTTO: put them on then

RUDOLF: I will

RUDOLF puts them on.

OTTO: you look ridiculous

RUDOLF: thank you.

Beat.

RUDOLF: 'when you say 1.2 kilos of uranium235 and I see the
numbers in front of me, but you could explain this figure
here…'

OTTO: they won't say that
they'll set up a separate committee to say all that

RUDOLF: what *will* they say?

Beat.

RUDOLF: what *will* they say?
an Austrian and a German delivering the biggest news of
defence this century
what will they say?

OTTO: they'll say…

A CLERK comes in.

He's rather formal in his manner, and comes over to the waiting men.

CLERK: the committee will be with you in just a few moments

OTTO: thank you

Beat.

The man still seems to hang around.

OTTO: I…

CLERK: do have your appointment card?

OTTO: appointment card?

CLERK: you were sent one
it's not important, it's just a regulation
an important regulation

RUDOLF: I thought it was just something to tell us the time of
the appointment

CLERK: not really no.

RUDOLF: oh

RUDOLF starts looking through his briefcase.

OTTO: shall we give you our names,

CLERK: I know your names.
you are Dr Frisch and Dr Peierls
delivering your memorandum
we're expecting you
the committee is expecting you
we wouldn't have let you across the threshold if we weren't
expecting you

OTTO: and if we don't have the appointment card?

CLERK: most people bring it.

    we find.

    to defence committee meetings

    most people remember that they have to bring a small card with them.

    it's not so much to carry

    and they understand the concept of security

    in war time

Beat.

OTTO and RUDOLF look through their pockets.

They have nothing.

OTTO: so what do we do now?

CLERK: you go home

OTTO: you're joking?

CLERK: As a rule I find I don't joke

OTTO: because we don't have the appointment card?

CLERK: it says, small letters I agree, but it says 'please bring this card with you'.

OTTO: we can't go home.

CLERK: 'failure to bring this card will result in not being allowed into the committee rooms'

OTTO: we've come all the way from Birmingham

CLERK: there's a nuisance

OTTO: I think they'll be interested in what we have to say

CLERK: we have regulations

    Whitehall isn't just a doctor's surgery, you can't just stroll in

RUDOLF: we have identification

we have our travel documents

CLERK: I'm sorry gentlemen
rules are rules

OTTO: go in there and tell the committee
tell them we're rather distracted, forgetful, we're just
scientists, we forgot our appointment cards

CLERK: they know the regulations better than I do
they made them after all

OTTO: could you go in there and give them the option?

CLERK: are you telling me what to do?

OTTO: I'm suggesting
I'm making a suggestion, based on an observation of the
situation and a prediction of possible outcomes

RUDOLF: Otto

OTTO: what?

There's a bit of stand-off between OTTO and the CLERK.

RUDOLF: I've found it

OTTO: what?

RUDOLF: sorry
there is a hole in the lining – I…sorry.

He gives it to the CLERK.

RUDOLF: no harm done

The CLERK goes away.

With a final dirty look.

OTTO hisses at RUDOLF.

OTTO: du Depp

RUDOLF: du drecksack

OTTO: du dreckiger Hurensohn!

RUDOLF: in English Otto please!

Beat.

OTTO is ready to give up.

OTTO: shall we go home?

Beat.

RUDOLF: you expect me to give you an answer?

OTTO: your glasses are broken, you won't be able to go over
the calculations,
your shirt is crumpled
my shoes look ridiculous
they don't trust us anyway
Strassman will get there within months, let him have it.

RUDOLF: and if we go home?

OTTO: the Germans will win the war. With almost certainty.

Beat.

OTTO: an appointment card honestly

RUDOLF: do you ever think you might talk too much?

OTTO: tcch.

Beat.

RUDOLF: what did you do on that Tuesday, after?

OTTO: what do you mean?

RUDOLF: the day of our discovery
when you went home that night

OTTO: I don't know made something to eat…?

RUDOLF: later then, when you were going to sleep, what were
you thinking?

OTTO: I was pleased Bohr got it wrong
the great Bohr, call it jealousy

RUDOLF: was that all you thought?

OTTO: are you asking me if I thought of anything beyond the science?
beyond the petty rivalry – ?

RUDOLF: yes

OTTO: no

RUDOLF: nothing?

OTTO: not a lot.

Beat.

RUDOLF: I went for a walk
I was as excited as you, more in fact
and Bohr, I agree, has it coming.
I like him in some ways but you can only be brilliant for so long
But then, later I was calm
it wasn't about Bohr anymore
I tried to explain the maths to my wife, she couldn't follow
it annoyed me that she couldn't follow
so I went back in to the lab.
I felt detached, like this work wasn't mine at all.
I double-checked the calculations
then I thought about the others

OTTO: the others?

RUDOLF: all the others we have worked with
Hahn, Heisenberg, Bohr of course, Strassman
all over Europe, working on the same thing
what it would mean to them
Fission has been this big beautiful thing,
for all of us

like magic
one element turning into another,
what could be more magic than that?

OTTO: agreed

RUDOLF: we've been like children, jumping up and down
look!
we can turn a uranium atom into a new element
we didn't need to worry.
yes there's energy given off, but the energy
you can't use it
not to any great extent
you would need 15 tonnes of uranium to use it
and then the rest, it would be far too heavy
so we're OK.
until
we found that that was based on a mistake
a miscalculation
that Bohr's predictions had been just a little out
no one can make a useful bomb when you start with 15
tonnes
but 1 kilogram
a bag of sugar?
you can make a bomb when you start with that

OTTO: you think too much
I just had something to eat and wrote to my aunt.

Beat.

OTTO: if we go home Strassman will get there first.
we found the mistake, and the others aren't stupid
Bohr himself will look again
it's weeks if not months
the brains of those men

RUDOLF: I know

I'm just saying

OTTO: what are you saying

Beat.

RUDOLF: I'm saying…
I don't know what I am saying.
I'm nervous.
I'm excited.
I'm German
my glasses have broken
that's all.

The CLERK comes back in.

CLERK: the committee will see you now

CALCULATED RISK
by Ron Hutchinson

First production

The Tricycle Theatre, London, 9th February 2012

Characters / Cast

CLEMENT ATTLEE	Michael Cochrane
JAMES BYRNES	David Yip
WILLIAM PENNEY	Rick Warden
FIELD MARSHAL GRIERSON	Simon Chandler
ERNEST BEVIN	Simon Rouse

Director   *Nicolas Kent*

The lights rise on British Prime Minister CLEMENT ATTLEE tensely facing the American Secretary of State JAMES BYRNES in an office in Potsdam for the August, 1945 Potsdam Conference.

ATTLEE: The what agreement?

BYRNES: The Quebec Agreement. August 1943.

ATTLEE: Between whom and about what?

BYRNES: The British government and ourselves concerning the building and use of an atomic bomb.

ATTLEE: I was the Deputy Prime Minister. Impossible that I wasn't party to it. If Mr. Churchill entered into a clandestine arrangement I don't see that I'm bound by it.

BYRNES: Whether you do or not, Prime Minister, we will hold you to it. The terms were that we never use it against each other and never use it without each other's consent.

ATTLEE: If I refuse to give that consent?

BYRNES: Your predecessor gave it before leaving office.

ATTLEE: If I retract it?

BYRNES: Too late. The weapons are being assembled; the targeting decisions have been made.

ATTLEE: Weapons?

BYRNES: We have enough material for two of the devices. Neither of which would have been possible, I might add, without your scientists and engineers.

ATTLEE: But not the then Deputy Prime Minister, it seems. I was to be kept in the dark.

Beat.

How big a bomb?

BYRNES: Big enough to end the war in one afternoon. That's why Truman is keeping it from the Russians until this Conference is over.

ATTLEE: Excuse me, Secretary Byrnes, for what might seem to be a levity – are you from Texas?

BYRNES: I'm from South Carolina and this is no exaggeration.

ATTLEE: Bomber Command killed tens of thousands a night in Dresden and Hamburg – you killed one hundred and eighty thousand in the fireball raid on Tokyo –

BYRNES: This is on a different scale. Something more like an earthquake or other natural disaster.

ATTLEE: Ready to be dropped on Japan in the name of the Allies – in my name – without them – me – having any say? Unacceptable. Totally unacceptable. It can't stand. No. Not to be countenanced. A postponement will be required, at the very least. A delay while His Majesty's Government – *this* government – considers its position.

BYRNES is unmoved.

BYRNES: We mean to bring the Pacific War to a close. We want our boys back. Preferably before Stalin finally declares war on Japan and tries to claim some share of the spoils. We believe it can be done in an afternoon. We will attempt that whether you like it or not. You should also know that the agreement also says that after the war the future use of this new source of power will be directed by the President of the United States. That is also something we will regard as binding.

ATTLEE: Was Truman aware of this agreement?

BYRNES: He's been made aware of it now that he's President. This message comes directly from him.

The mission is operational in a very few hours. There is a Texan phrase I heard a young Congressman name of Lyndon Johnson employ once. A Southern gentleman should not use it to an English one but in view of the urgency – Time to piss or get off the pot –

Before ATTLEE can respond there's a white flash and a deep rumble and papers fly off the desk as the screen shows the mushroom cloud rising above Hiroshima.

Blackout.

We hear Vera Lynn singing 'When The Lights Go On Again' as the lights rise on ATTLEE in a small room in Downing Street with the civilian scientist WILLIAM PENNEY and the uniformed FIELD MARSHAL GRIERSON. It's a few days later.

PENNEY: The initial test at Alamogordo – the dry run – gave us some idea of its power – a crater ten feet deep and a thousand feet wide – the shock wave felt a hundred miles away – but last month, over Nagasaki – it was even more devastating than one could have hoped for.

ATTLEE: You were actually there, Doctor Penney?

PENNEY: I begged a ride as an observer in the second plane.

ATTLEE: You mean you've seen two atomic bombs go off?

PENNEY: I'm an expert in wave dynamics – I thought that the hills around those cities would help focus the blasts –

ATTLEE: And kill more people?

PENNEY: That was a political decision. I just gave my scientific advice.

ATTLEE: We've another decision to make now. Whether to go ahead with our own bomb.

PENNEY: It is in many ways our bomb already, Prime Minister. Leó Szilárd realized that a chain reaction would be possible while walking in Southampton Row. Otto Frisch and Rudolf Peierls were working at Birmingham University when they warned the coalition government that a weapon could be built. We just couldn't afford to build it, which is where the Americans came in.

GRIERSON: But does that mean that we have to spend the millions upon millions it's going to take to build our own, now?

ATTLEE: I would have thought the Armed Forces would have wanted it without question, Field Marshal.

GRIERSON: Hiroshima and Nagasaki showed that Penney and his fellow scientists have handed the world a weapon that can only be used against civilian populations. Non-combatants. The innocent.

The laws of war? The understanding that even in battle there have to be limits? What happened to them?

Even if you agree to it, where will the millions it takes come from? If we find them who gets to control it? The Air Force? The Navy? Us?

As a soldier, as someone whose trade is war, I'm arguing, sir, not to be saddled with this odious thing. I'd rather resign than bloody my hands with it.

PENNEY: I won't get into an argument about the morality of using it – talk to a Chaplain about that –

GRIERSON: My brother-in-law was due to be on a troop ship heading to the Far East this month. He's alive only because we won't have to invade the Japanese mainland now. I leave all sentiment or morality about dead Japanese aside. I worry about this solely as a professional soldier.

PENNEY: It works. That's what was as astonishing as those mushroom clouds. *It works.* It was by no means certain that it would. That was one of the reasons for not inviting Japanese observers to the test site. What if it fizzled? Or they thought it was a hoax? And if it worked, why not use it? Why throw all those hundreds of millions of dollars away to no purpose?

ATTLEE: We're not arguing about whether it should have been used on Japan – that horse has left the stable –

GRIERSON: With all due respect, sir – doesn't what happened a few days ago inform the decision you have to make now?

ATTLEE: What can that argument always be save *I raise you one dead American soldier, you raise me one dead Japanese civilian?* It goes nowhere. Whether you approve of the incineration of two cities filled mostly with civilians to allegedly shorten the war – that seems to me to be a matter of individual temperament. I can't waste my time on it. What concerns me now are the practical consequences for the British government.

Without them noticing the door opens and the Foreign Secretary ERNEST BEVIN enters.

GRIERSON: If one of those consequences is having the country bankrupted to pay for a weapon we will never use –

ATTLEE: Never use?

GRIERSON: Could you have dropped one of those bombs on Berlin or Hamburg, sir? Really? Had it been in your power to do so?

PENNEY: If it had been the only way to stop the Germans dropping one on London or Manchester –

ATTLEE: *(Impatiently.)* That war is won. Do get on. Help me. Guide my thinking. Inform me. Argue it each way. I must get this right. It's the next war I have to worry about. Moscow and Kiev are more to the point.

BEVIN: I've talked with Molotov and Voroshilov and the other buggers. You don't get much change out of a pound with those boys.

The others turn to see BEVIN striding in with burly energy and a strong West of England accent –

We are dealing with gangsters, not gentlemen, when we talk about Uncle Joe and his gang, let us remember that. I know that if he ever did get his hands on us it would be our esteemed colleagues of the Parliamentary Labour Party who'd get the rubber truncheons and bullet in the back of the head first. Am I right, Prime Minister?

ATTLEE: It's the Social Democrats they're putting against the wall in Eastern and Central Europe, yes.

BEVIN: The only thing that will impress Moscow is a bloody big bomb of our own with a Union Jack on top of it.

ATTLEE: I'm not sure if the Field Marshal sees it quite that way.

BEVIN: Of course he does. How could he see it any other way? We have to make it Labour Party policy that we have an independent nuclear weapon, even if the Labour Party isn't to know about it until it's too late.

GRIERSON: I'm here to persuade you that we don't want this weapon at any price. That we can't afford to build it and that if we do it puts all the big decisions in the hands of – well – civilians like you. Politicians. Not professional military men.

BEVIN: Like the ones at Singapore who pointed the guns in the wrong direction? Had to be saved by rowing boats at Dunkirk?

GRIERSON: We did win the war.

BEVIN: We ended up on the winning side. A bit different. I've known two world wars. Each time we had to go begging to the Yanks. Not any more. Not with our own bomb. This changes everything. You know that, Prime Minister. You were a soldier and a bloody good one –

ATTLEE: But if it is in the last analysis a means of spreading terror through mass destruction –

PENNEY: And if that is how the wars of the future are to be fought?

BEVIN: What's the alternative to having our own bomb? Hiding behind the skirts of the Yanks? We'd be taking dictation from Uncle Sam about everything – *everything* – domestic as well as foreign policy – as the price for our security.

ATTLEE: I wonder how many of the Party we can bring there with us, however – the pacifist wing –

BEVIN: You can be a socialist without being a pacifist. There's one standing right here.

GRIERSON: I said I wouldn't argue a moral case but perhaps I have to. With your permission, Prime Minister –

He turns to PENNEY –

Perhaps you shouldn't have made your peace so easily with your targeting decision. Perhaps it wasn't a simple scientific problem. Perhaps you should examine your role in a mass murder which, had we lost, would have seen you put on trial as a war criminal.

As they react –

That has implications for everybody in this room. At Nuremberg we're not going to allow the Nazis to claim they were following orders, are we?

PENNEY: I worked with numbers. Formulae. Drew graphs. Projected possibilities. Pointed out statistical outcomes.

GRIERSON: Real people died.

ATTLEE: We were at war.

GRIERSON: We will constantly be at war if we build this thing and I wonder how much in charge of it you'll really be – even as Prime Minister. The programme to build it, work out a means to deliver it, try to decide who to use it against and when and how – it will take on a life of its own. Once we build it we will never be able to give it up.

BEVIN: Cock. Utter cock. If we want to look Uncle Joe in the eye, stand toe to toe with the Yanks we need our own bomb and we need it now.

ATTLEE: At what cost? Bankrupting ourselves? Morally as well as financially?

BEVIN: How can you send me into the conference chamber without this to back me up? Especially if the Russians get theirs?

ATTLEE: You know how much of a bad way we're in. You've seen the figures. The cost of building it –

BEVIN: The price of not building it?

GRIERSON: You've been talking about a National Health Service – changing the education system – making sure that this time there really are homes fit for heroes to come back to – can you afford to do both?

PENNEY: May I come in here? Add some larger perspective? I have a print in my office. It shows Galileo in the hands of the Inquisition. Even after the threat of torture led him to recant the claim that the earth circles the sun he's supposed to have murmured *It still moves*. That was the moment in which the modern world began.

He indicates the fire –

It ultimately meant that we went from a world lit by fire to electricity and the radio and now television –

GRIERSON: And mustard gas and the bomber and the atomic bomb –

PENNEY: So are you proposing we find some way to stop science in its tracks? How exactly would that work?

BEVIN: If the cat's out of the bag it's out of the bag.

ATTLEE: I think the Field Marshal is arguing that it could still be stuffed back in. That before it gets more than its whiskers out we still have a chance.

GRIERSON: Doctor Penney asks us to trust the scientists. But this thing doesn't just have the potential to change the world – it could bring it to an end.

BEVIN: More cock.

ATTLEE: An exaggeration, surely.

GRIERSON: I've read the file – as much of it as has been declassified. I don't pretend to understand the maths but isn't it true –

He turns to PENNEY –

– that you weren't at all certain that a chain reaction could be contained?

PENNEY looks uncomfortable –

PENNEY: It was, yes, theoretically, mathematically possible that it couldn't be stopped; that once we exploded the bomb the process would go on and on until it consumed every atom in the planet. But –

GRIERSON: But you went ahead anyway. That's my point, Prime Minister. They knew it might bring an end to everything and these are the people you're being asked to give carte blanche to? Without any check on their ambition or recklessness?

PENNEY: President Truman was aware of the risks and made a very brave decision.

ATTLEE: Or a damn fool one but if the cat really is out of the bag, paws and tail – ? If the Russians build theirs? How can I send my Foreign Secretary to face them without our own bomb to back him up?

BEVIN: *(To GRIERSON.)* We're a very small island, a few miles away from a Europe which might well be under the heel of the Red Army in the next few months. You really want to leave us naked?

ATTLEE: President Truman had to make a decision. I reluctantly have to agree that he made the right one. The world didn't end. We must hope that we keep getting it right. What else can we do?

PENNEY: It may well be that the decision was already made for him when Rutherford laid the foundations of nuclear physics or Galileo those of the modern world. The thing was possible. Therefore it was indeed inevitable. The part that Truman played – that I played – that you will be called on to play – that may be inevitable, too.

GRIERSON: We have free will. As a nation as well as individually. We can see the brink and pull back in time.

BEVIN: Free will? Galileo? I'm a practical man –

ATTLEE: Indeed you are, Foreign Secretary.

BEVIN: read my election material –

ATTLEE: That's why you're so valuable to us – but I'm very conscious now of just how much this thing has changed – well – everything. The old way of not just fighting but conducting the affairs of nations – it's out of the window. For good or ill – probably ill – we have to start from scratch. It's as if until now we've been fighting with bows and arrows and now we have gunpowder. The responsibility for getting it right frankly terrifies me – but I do intend to get it right. How often does something on a scale such as this come along? What did we go into public life for if it wasn't for a moment like this?

BEVIN: I got into trade unionism because I saw men who had been broken by the First War thrown on the scrap heap of the Slump. I fought for them and I swore there'd be no more war to do that to another generation of working men and then Hitler came along. I admire those who stayed pacifist in the face of his crimes but I went the other way. So what do I do when a Penney here and his pals hand me a weapon that might just, might just be so terrible that it brings all wars to an end?

GRIERSON: You can't possibly believe that.

PENNEY: I should think he's seen the photographs of Hiroshima and Nagasaki after the blasts.

BEVIN: I can imagine London or Manchester or Leeds looking like that. I can only hope the Americans think of Washington and New York when they see them. That Stalin thinks of Moscow and Kiev. That might be our best – our only guarantee that things are going to be different now. Could it be possible? That war could be so terrible that it would outlaw itself?

ATTLEE: We were told that about the machine gun, the battleship, the torpedo, the tank and aerial bombardment. We ended up in a worse mess than ever.

PENNEY: Wittgenstein said that if someone tells you that two and two equals five there's a problem but you're still talking about the same thing. If he tells you that two and two equals ninety-seven, you are basically buggered. Excuse my French. Two and two does now equal ninety-seven. Everything has changed. This is not just a bigger, bangier bomb. It's different, fundamentally different. Not an evolution, a revolution. Not a change in magnitude, one in kind. Not just another day but a new dawn on a new planet. I know that. Better than any of you. I was there. On the ground at Alamogordo. In the air over Nagasaki.

He turns to GRIERSON –

You've made your feelings toward me as a man as well as a scientist very plain – but what if I helped do what no one in uniform could ever do? Scare mankind out of its habit of resolving disputes by violence?

GRIERSON: After what I've seen I wish to God no one would ever pick up another weapon again. For any reason. But you and your accomplices rearranged the atom. You didn't change human nature.

PENNEY is angered –

PENNEY: My *accomplices* brought the most terrible war in history to an end. It took us seconds to do it.

BEVIN: Something that you'd been trying and failing to do for six years. Even with the help of Uncle Sam.

ATTLEE: And it was a politician who had the courage to say Yes. Truman may have been a bankrupt draper from a small town in Missouri who people thought wasn't up to the job but he had the guts to do it.

GRIERSON: Even though there was a possibility the Japanese were on the point of surrender anyway?

ATTLEE: Nobody can say that for sure.

GRIERSON: You're a practical man, Mr. Bevin – you'd agree that using it was as much to cower the Russians as persuade the Japanese?

BEVIN: Truman and Churchill are responsible for that –

GRIERSON: But you must see the implications. We killed all those civilians – men, women and children – to make a political point, not primarily to achieve a military objective. They made their decision and, yes, they will have to live with it –

Turning to ATTLEE –

– but what about the ones you might be forced to live with, in the years ahead?

ATTLEE: I was elected to make those decisions.

BEVIN: In a landslide.

GRIERSON: But now we know what kind of weapon it is? Now we've seen it's so much more terrible than we could have imagined?

BEVIN: It would be the responsibility of anyone who sat in that office to weigh its use. Not you. Not even Doctor Penney.

ATTLEE: And a heavy responsibility it would be.

GRIERSON: It only makes sense as a weapon if you use it ahead of the other side. Even Penney would agree with that. It's a knockout blow or nothing. You're being asked not only to be ready to commit mass murder but to do it on a probability – *a probability* of attack.

BEVIN looks as if he's had enough –

BEVIN: I would like the other world, Yesterday's World I would. I'm sure the Prime Minister would, too. The one without the bomb. Things would be simpler in it but we can't ever get it back. This is the world that was made by the bomb that was dropped by the plane that we built on one day in August in 1945 and that's all you can say.

GRIERSON: No. I think you have to add *This is the child who was burned to ash in the world that we made by the bomb that was dropped by the plane that we built on one day in August 1945.*

PENNEY: But also *This is the soldier whose life was saved by the child who was burned to ash in the world that we made by the bomb.*

They're angrily face to face and ATTLEE steps in –

ATTLEE: And now I have to struggle to make sense of it all in practical political terms as well as military and moral ones. One almost wishes Mr. Churchill was still resident here; that one's role would be to judge his actions rather than determine the right response oneself but I shall do my best.

He stands to show the meeting is over –

You've all been very helpful, gentlemen. Now I think you must leave me to think it through.

Scrupulously polite, he shakes hands with PENNEY –

Please hold yourself in readiness, Doctor Penney. In one way or another I feel the nation may call on you again. In peace, one hopes – but it might be, alas, in war.

PENNEY exits as ATTLEE shakes GRIERSON's hand –

I do hope you won't resign, Field Marshal. I understand the reservations of the military. But you are clear, I hope, that in our system of government the civilians give the orders and the soldiers determine the means to carry them out.

He holds the handshake a beat longer than necessary to emphasise the point before letting GRIERSON exit.

BEVIN: A couple more points –

ATTLEE reaches for his hand –

ATTLEE: I couldn't possibly keep you from the pressing demands of the most important office of state after mine, Foreign Secretary. Eastern Europe, Palestine, the Ruhr, India – they all cry out for your immediate attention –

BEVIN: I just need to make sure that –

ATTLEE: *Immediate* attention.

A brief battle of wills between the two men, then BEVIN backs down, heads away, then pauses –

BEVIN: Folk say to me it can't be easy for poor old Attlee, stepping into the shoes of a Churchill. I tell them *Wait and see what size boots he's wearing.*

He exits and for a moment ATTLEE is alone with his decision. Then the lights snap out as we hear Flanagan and Allen's 'There's a Boy Coming Home on Leave'.

The lights rise on BYRNES, intently reading a two and a half page memo. As he does so he mutters approval –

BYRNES: Yes…yes…my God yes…

ATTLEE enters as he finishes the document.

Extraordinary, sir. Quite extraordinary. In one go you seem to have grasped everything that this weapon means.

ATTLEE: Texan exaggeration or Southern courtesy?

BYRNES: The plain truth –

He indicates various paragraphs –

The conception of war we've become accustomed to is now out of date...scientists agree we cannot stop the march of discovery... any attempt to keep it a secret is futile...must face stark reality... essential to end wars...banish it from people's minds and the calculations of governments.

ATTLEE takes the pages from him, reads one of the final paragraphs –

ATTLEE: *No government has ever been placed in such a position as is ours today. The governments of the UK and the USA are responsible as never before for the future of the human race.*

I trust you will take those sentiments back to Washington and make sure they are acted on, Mr. Secretary. You must. *You must.*

BYRNES: How could I not?

ATTLEE: Including bringing Stalin into this? Tying his hands before he gets his own bomb?

BYRNES: I can't give any guarantees –

ATTLEE: It has to be done.

BYRNES: That might be a tough sell in Congress –

ATTLEE: It's a time for boldness, Mr. Byrnes. For the same decisiveness which ended the war at a stroke. Which cut me out of the Agreement made in Quebec. We either put in place an international mechanism to master this thing or it will master us. We and our policies, internal and external will be slaves to it forever.

BYRNES: I will do my best.

ATTLEE: I'm sure you will. I'm sure President Truman will listen. He has to. Everything is at stake now. Civilization, the very existence of mankind. *Everything.* You'll appreciate how hard it is for British reserve to even say that.

BYRNES: Indeed I do –

He turns towards the door, hesitates –

It would help if there was a little more clarity on one issue.

He indicates the pages of the document –

Nowhere in there does it say whether you'll go ahead with your own bomb.

ATTLEE: That is not the purpose of the document.

BYRNES: No, but –

ATTLEE: It is my personal reflection and warning.

BYRNES: And greatly to be appreciated. It would still, however, be useful to have some idea of where you might be heading. If you do indeed intend to claim a right to develop your own nuclear policy.

ATTLEE: That would be a Cabinet matter. Our system is not – not yet anyway – a presidential one.

BYRNES: All the same – some indication from the First among Equals –

ATTLEE: It may be, of course, that a small group within the Cabinet would be a better way to handle things; without troubling the other members of it.

BYRNES: You'd keep it secret even from the rest of them?

ATTLEE: As so much was kept from me? This whole enterprise, begun in so much secrecy, seems to entangle everyone who has dealings with it in a nest of secrets, denials, deceptions, obfuscations and outright lies. It's as if the truth about it recoils from the light – if that doesn't sound too Churchillian – a fault I have seldom been taxed with.

ATTLEE takes out his pipe, starts to pack it with tobacco –

ATTLEE: *(Cont'd.)* I couldn't possibly allow you to leave here with any intimation that I will set His Majesty's Government to one course of action over the other –

BYRNES: Of course not –

ATTLEE: Especially as the Agreement seems to forbid me doing so without President Truman's fiat –

BYRNES: It does, yes –

He's listening intently, knowing that he's being told to read between the lines.

ATTLEE: Just as you can't categorically, as an honorable man, assure me that now that the war is won your country won't retreat into isolationism again – leaving us to fend for ourselves –

BYRNES: I can hardly see that happening.

ATTLEE: Not in the immediate afterglow of a joint victory, no – but in a few months or years?

He takes out his matches –

I don't suppose you follow football, do you? Our kind of football?

BYRNES: No.

ATTLEE: It will be a great help to morale when we can get the grounds open again. Get the players demobbed, into their kit and onto the field. At last it will look as if we're getting back to normal.

He lights the pipe –

There's a young chap name of Stanley Matthews. You won't have heard of him but he's getting a lot of attention. He may well prove to be one of the greatest players of the game who ever lived. I suppose one could ask him to kick a football around in the park on a Sunday afternoon but I imagine what he'd really want would be a crack at a first-rate team like Blackpool or Stoke or Bolton Wanderers. To test himself against the best. Show what he's got. Get an international cap. Play for his country. Take on the world. Prove that he has it in him; he's someone to be reckoned with. In his own right. Through his own abilities. Not simply standing in the shadow of someone else. That he has what it takes. Personally.

Yes.

I should think that's what he would want. Wouldn't you? If you were First Division material? And wanted everyone to be aware of it?

As they face each other the lights fade on them as we hear The Andrews Sisters singing their 1945 hit 'Rum and Coca Cola'.

End.

SEVEN JOYS
by Lee Blessing

First production
   The Tricycle Theatre, London, 9th February 2012

Characters / Cast

CAL American	Rick Warden
HENRY Englishman	Michael Cochrane
SLAVA Russian	Simon Rouse
WEI Chinese	David Yip
MARIANNE French	Shereen Martin

   Various offstage voices

   Director   *Nicolas Kent*

Setting
   The action takes place in a Gentlemen's club,
   from 1945 to nearly the present day.

A room in an exclusive Gentlemen's club. A leather club chair dominates. The only other piece of furniture is a small table on which a glowing, egg-like object – perhaps the size of a goose egg – sits in a cylindrical base.

CAL enters, wearing a smoking jacket. He stops, looks around and breathes a sigh of profound satisfaction.

CAL: Listen to that. Now *that* is silence.

CAL circles the room once, very slowly, taking in the silence. Finally he focuses on the club chair. His brow knits. He looks closer at the seat of the chair.

Henry – !!

HENRY enters quickly. His manner is overly ingratiating.

HENRY: Yes, sir?

CAL: What in hell is *that?*

HENRY: *(Inspecting the chair carefully.)* It would appear to be… I think I'd have to call it, um…uh…

CAL: What?!

HENRY: A spot. A little…not absolutely positive… Waxy, though; I think perhaps when I was moving a candle –

CAL: A candle?! What century do you think we're in?

HENRY: You wanted a certain ambience –

CAL: I don't want *can*dles. No wonder this place is dark all the time.

HENRY: Mystery, you said. I was just trying to create a sense of…

Starting out.

I'll get some lamps.

CAL: Aren't you forgetting something?

HENRY: What?

As CAL looks at the chair.

Oh! Yes, of course. Can't have you sitting on that.

HENRY hurries back, produces a letter opener from his pocket and carefully removes the spot of wax.

CAL: You carry a letter opener around with you?

HENRY: I need to. For all the applications you're receiving.

CAL: Applications?

HENRY: For admission to the club. Everyone wants to get in. Especially Slava. He sends one every day.

CAL: Fuckin' Russian thug. Like I'm going to help him. You've seen what he does to people.

HENRY: I have indeed. Still, he's highly motivated – on this issue, at least. He's becoming something of a pest. It's just paranoia, I suppose. Still, considering what he's gone through recently...

CAL: What?! What has *he* gone through?

HENRY: I mean, that German fellow was awfully hard on him. And, um...and he's lost a lot of friends recently.

CAL: 'Cause he's a thug!

HENRY: And now, on top of all of it, there's this...this club which he...can't get in.

CAL: Precisely. That was the whole intention.

HENRY: Yes, of course. Certainly the only logical rationale for creating it, I suppose. Still –

CAL: What?! Spit it out.

HENRY: It tends to strike a good deal of fear into people.

CAL: And thank God for that. Henry, listen to me. For the first time in history a club like this exists. And people are afraid. They're afraid like nobody's ever been afraid before.

HENRY: Yes, Sir. Yes, they are.

CAL: They're afraid of what I might do.

HENRY: Yes.

CAL: 'Cause I could kill them. By the millions. Like that. First time in history.

HENRY: Yes.

CAL: Kill 'em all. I could even kill you.

(After a beat, laughing.) Not that I would, of course.

HENRY: *(Laughing weakly.)* No, no – of course not.

CAL: Wouldn't kill Henry. Wouldn't kill my little Prince Hal. What sense would that make?

HENRY: None at all.

CAL: After I went to all that trouble to save you?

HENRY: Right.

CAL: *(Suddenly dead serious.)* Because I did save you. Without me you'd all be saying, 'Please fuck me in the ass' in German right now.

HENRY: Yes. I imagine we would.

CAL: And?

HENRY: And we're, um…we're forever grateful, of course.

CAL: I went to lengths. Great lengths to save the world. Developed massive destructive power. Found the inner wisdom to contain it. I have inner wisdom.

HENRY: Yes, you do. And we…we bank on that.

CAL: You should. Hell, that's why there's only one member of this club. Because you know what my inner wisdom tells me? It tells me that no one else *has* inner wisdom.

HENRY: I see.

CAL: Not even you, Henry. Not way, way inside where it counts. That's why you're not a member of the club.

HENRY: I see.

CAL: But I do let you in here, don't I? Even without inner wisdom, there's something special about you.

HENRY: Thanks, Cal.

CAL: And, no matter how small the membership is, we still need a staff.

HENRY: You're very kind. Actually Cal, I was wondering about my wage…

CAL: Too low?

HENRY: It's very hard to make ends meet.

CAL: Need a loan?

HENRY: I'd hoped for a higher salary.

CAL: You got it. Things are going good right now.

HENRY: Thank you.

CAL: And hell – who else am I going to hire? You're the only guy I can trust. Look at the rest of them out there.

Drawing aside a curtain, looking outside.

Skulking around, trying to figure a way in. They think it's safer in here. It's not, though. Know why?

HENRY: Why?

CAL: 'Cause if this place ever gets a member who has no inner wisdom, we'll all be in deep shit. Whether I like it or not, I'm the only one responsible enough to *be* in this club.

HENRY: You bear a heavy load.

CAL: Tell me about it.

Sound of a window shattering in another room. HARRY starts toward the noise, but CAL holds him by the arm. Sound of heavy footfalls. SLAVA, dressed in a Soviet General's uniform of the late 1940s, enters and takes a wide stance before them.

SLAVA: Hello.

HENRY: Slava, what on earth are you doing?! This is a private club.

SLAVA: The most private. I know.

CAL: You might have knocked. You didn't have to break a window to get in.

SLAVA: I wasn't trying to get in. I was trying to get out. I sneaked in here days ago. A friend of yours slipped me the plans to the building.

CAL: Who?!

SLAVA: What's it matter? Once you're in, you're in, eh? What's for dinner?

HENRY: Not so fast. You haven't proven you have any right here at all.

SLAVA pulls from his pocket an egg like the one on the small table. It does not however glow.

That's not proof!

SLAVA flips a small switch at the base of the egg. It now glows.

Oh... Oh, dear.

SLAVA produces a ring like the one in which CAL's egg sits and places the new glowing egg next to CAL's.

SLAVA: You have very smart friends, Cal. And they like to talk.

CAL: Why were you sneaking out?

SLAVA: I have to go to the lumber store. This place is too small. I need to add another wing.

HENRY: I don't understand. If you had this –

Indicating SLAVA's egg.

Why didn't you just come in? Why'd you have to sneak around?

SLAVA: I'm sneaky. You have problem with that?

HENRY: No, no. I merely –

SLAVA: What are *you* doing here?

CAL: He's staff.

SLAVA: *(Suspicious.)* Sure he is.

CAL: I'm not sure I want you doing a big remodeling job –

SLAVA: Get used to it. I spent 1,485 sleepless nights since your little tap-dance on Tojo, and I've got news for you. I'm going to make new wing just as big as this whole building. If you make building bigger, I make wing bigger, understand? Just as big as you – *always.*

HENRY: I see your personality hasn't changed.

SLAVA: *What?!*

CAL: Slava, it's my duty to welcome you to the club – since, of course, I have no alternative. However I would like to impress upon you the continuing importance of keeping the membership to an absolute minimum. Therefore the only faces I want to see in here are you, me and Henry, of course.

SLAVA: And Wei.

CAL: Who?

SLAVA: The cook. Well, caterer. He has a restaurant on the other side of town. It's called Seven Joys.

CAL: Seven – ?

SLAVA: Wonderful food. You'll see.

CAL: You want to bring him in *here?* I already have a cook: Henry.

SLAVA: Henry? My condolences.

HENRY: What do you mean by that?

SLAVA: Besides, I only like Chinese food. I can put a kitchen in my wing. No problem.

CAL: I think there *is* a problem –

SLAVA: Why? You have Henry, I have Wei. Here, I'll show you.

(Calling.) Wei!

CAL: He's here?!

WEI enters in a richly appointed, traditional Chinese robe. Smiling, he bows. SLAVA helps him remove the robe. Underneath, he wears the uniform of the People's Republic of China.

SLAVA: I admit, he's a bit of a protégé. He likes me, what can I say?

CAL: And he's here to cook?

SLAVA: That's all. You won't even notice him.

CAL: You run a restaurant?

WEI: Oh, yes. It's called Seven Joys. First joy: Workers' paradise – everyone works together. Second joy –

CAL: I don't have to hear 'em all right now –

SLAVA: Better not to stop him once he's started.

WEI: Second joy – if you don't work together, you fall off the roof. Third joy… I forget third joy. Fourth joy:

Embracing SLAVA.

We have a big new friend. Fifth joy: access to this beautiful building.

HENRY: Don't get too attached.

WEI: Why are *you* attached?

CAL: Calm down, both of you.

WEI: Sixth joy: loyal neighbors.

CAL: Who's he talking about?

SLAVA: Nobody. Customers in his restaurant. He demands a lot of loyalty.

WEI: *(Forcefully.)* They eat with *me!* And sometimes we even serve Korean food.

SLAVA: Yes, Wei. We understand. Let's get started on the new wing.

WEI: *(As they turn to go.)* Seventh joy: the future.

CAL: 'The future'? What's he talking about?

SLAVA: I don't know; he likes the future.

> *(To WEI.)* Come on! There's a lot to do.

> *SLAVA and WEI exit, arm in arm.*

HENRY: I don't like this at all.

CAL: Neither do I. Here.

> *CAL hands HENRY a non-glowing egg-like object – perhaps the size of a chicken egg.*

HENRY: What's this?

CAL: You know.

HENRY: *(Highly complimented.)* Really? Thank you, Cal.

> *Inspecting it for a switch, finding none.*

> There's no…you know.

CAL: Work on it.

HENRY: I certainly will.

CAL: Something tells me that dealing with Slava's going to take a team effort.

HENRY: I'll get right on it.

HENRY exits, holding the egg out in front of him. CAL stares around the room. Suddenly sounds of a commotion come from the kitchen: crashing pans, breaking crockery, etc.

CAL: What in hell is *that!?*

CAL rushes off, towards the kitchen. The sounds get louder and worse. Finally, CAL and WEI emerge from the kitchen, fighting. They grab at each other's throat as they struggle. Perhaps one has a steel ladle, the other a meat tenderizer. SLAVA is right behind them, hands on them both, trying to separate them.

WEI: You keep away from him!

CAL: He attacked me! He's an aggressive little shit!

WEI: He's my friend!

SLAVA: Stop fighting!

CAL: You have no right to have him in there!

WEI: It's *kim chee* night! I've got to have him!

HENRY rushes in.

HENRY: What's going on?!

CAL: Help me!

HENRY struggles with CAL against WEI as SLAVA tries to pull both of them apart.

SLAVA: *Let…go!*

WEI: No!

CAL: Not till he does!

CAL picks up his glowing egg.

WEI: I dare you to use it!

CAL: I will use it!

SLAVA: *(Picking up his own glowing egg.)* And I will use mine!

A standoff. Slowly, CAL and WEI let each other go, one hand at a time. HENRY also lets go. CAL keeps his eye on SLAVA the whole time. WEI brushes himself off and addresses CAL.

WEI: No *kim chee* for you.

(Pointing at HENRY.) Or you.

WEI exits back into the kitchen. SLAVA and CAL carefully and simultaneously set down their eggs.

SLAVA: It's new world, big boy. Think before you act.

CAL: You think.

SLAVA: *(Starting out.)* No, *you* think.

CAL: *You* think!

(As SLAVA exits.) I'm getting a bigger egg!

HENRY: Awfully aggressive, isn't he?

CAL: How are you coming on with that one I gave you?

HENRY: Good news.

HENRY pulls out his egg and switches it on.

CAL: Good. That'll make 'em think.

HENRY: Are you really going to get a bigger egg?

CAL: Oh, yeah.

As HENRY sets his newly-glowing egg on the table.

Oh…yeah.

Blackout. Sounds of construction – SLAVA's building his wing. The sounds grow louder and more complex: piles being driven, jackhammers, trucks' back-up alarms, wood being sawn, etc. Finally, the sounds abate. Silence.

Lights come up on the same room. Now there are two large, leather club chairs that frame the small table, plus one smaller club chair. On the table now are one goose egg-sized glowing egg and two ostrich-sized glowing eggs.

SLAVA, now in a business suit, and CAL sit in the two large chairs. HENRY sits in the smaller one. They're having brandy after a large meal. They might be smoking.

SLAVA: How was your *kim chee?*

CAL: Passable.

HENRY: I'm getting tired of Asian food. Can't we have some haggis?

They look at HENRY and shake their heads despairingly.

I have the right to my opinion. I'm a member in good standing here.

SLAVA: *(Pointing at the glowing goose egg.)* Not standing very tall, though.

HENRY: Tall enough. In concert, anyway. With… Cal here.

SLAVA: *(To CAL.)* You and your minions.

CAL: Look who's talking. Let's be civil, gentlemen. I think we should congratulate ourselves on having found some strategic equipoise at long last. No one has joined the club in – what is it now?

SLAVA: 2,680 restful nights *and* counting.

CAL: Well, no matter what our disagreements, I can certainly drink to that.

HENRY: As can I.

SLAVA: As can –

SLAVA stops in mid-sentence, hearing something. It's the sound of high heels on a marble floor. All three men look anxiously offstage toward the front foyer. After a moment an extremely attractive, elegantly stylish woman, MARIANNE, enters.

MARIANNE: *Bon soir.*

SLAVA: Oh, crap.

MARIANNE: *Je m'appelle Marianne.*

The three men look at each other. HENRY rises awkwardly and takes her proffered hand.

HENRY: *Enchante.*

SLAVA: What are you doing here?

She smiles graciously, opens a small clutch purse and takes from it a goose egg-sized object which does not glow. She flips a switch, and it glows.

Bozhe moi!

She places the glowing egg on the table, next to HENRY's, then looks around.

HENRY: *(Offering his seat.)* Oh, please –

MARIANNE: *Merci.*

HENRY exits.

CAL: *(Who has not risen.)* You only speak French? 'Cause that's not going to work around here.

MARIANNE: Oh – no, no. I speak English as well. When I am…forced.

SLAVA: Why in hell are you here?

CAL: Easy, Slava. It's a good question, though. Why go to all the trouble of –

Gesturing at her egg.

You know. I mean, shoot – look at the table. I had you covered.

MARIANNE: Perhaps. But I prefer things this way.

HENRY drags in another leather chair, the size of the one in which MARIANNE now sits. He parks it next to hers and sits.

CAL: I still don't get it.

SLAVA: And I don't like it!

MARIANNE: It's nothing. Simply a matter of security, I suppose. It always feels safer to have a small *Force de frappe, n'est-ce pas?*

CAL: A what?

MARIANNE: A strike force.

SLAVA: Who do you plan to strike?

MARIANNE: No one, with luck. It's only to make people think twice.

Nudging her egg closer to CAL's on the table.

You, for example – are you thinking twice?

CAL: I had no idea you wanted this, um…this frap thing, Marianne.

MARIANNE: Really? I've been complaining about it for some time. You didn't hear me?

CAL: How could I? You were outside.

MARIANNE: And now I'm inside. Can you hear me now?

CAL: Yeah, yeah – I get it.

MARIANNE: So. What's for dinner?

WEI enters, carrying a small pad and pencil.

WEI: Good evening. May I have your orders?

MARIANNE: Oh, yes. Of course. I'll have three to four hundred active warheads, split between submarine-launched and medium-range, air-to-surface missiles.

WEI: Very good. And you?

HENRY: Not feeling all that peckish. I'll have pretty much the same: two to four hundred, bombers and submarines.

WEI: Excellent. And you?

SLAVA: Tonight I'm very hungry. 45,000 warheads – mostly active.

WEI: Ooh, that's a lot. Will you want a doggy bag?

SLAVA: No. And I want multiple delivery options.

WEI: Very well. And you?

CAL: *(Of SLAVA.)* I'll have what he's having.

WEI: Some big eaters in this club. Thank you so much.

As WEI turns to go, he places a goose-sized egg – unglowing – on the table between SLAVA's and the others, then heads towards the kitchen.

CAL: What the hell's that?!

WEI: Nothing.

SLAVA: What *is* it?!

WEI: Nothing. It's not even glowing. Oh, that's right! I forgot.

WEI claps his hands. His egg glows. WEI exits. CAL turns on SLAVA.

CAL: Did you know he was going to do that?!

SLAVA: Not this soon…

MARIANNE: This can't be good.

HENRY: I don't like it at all. Things are getting out of hand. I mean, if the help can worm its way into full membership –

MARIANNE: He's not the 'help'.

HENRY: He's helping us. He's staff, isn't he?

CAL: We've got to do something. We've got to nip this in the bud.

SLAVA: Absolutely.

CAL: Let's sign an agreement. No more members. Five, no more.

SLAVA: Five.

MARIANNE: Like the fingers on your hand.

HENRY: It's almost mystical.

CAL: Yeah, and we'll make all those bozos out there sign it, too. Five's the magic number. What do you say? Everyone agreed?

THE OTHERS: *(Together.)* Agreed!

WEI re-enters, dragging with him a very small club chair.

WEI: *(As he sits.)* I forgot to mention. Since I'll be out here more, I've brought in some help in the kitchen. Hard workers. You won't even notice them.

CAL: Who are they? Chinese, like you?

WEI: Mmm...Asian.

Brightly, as they all regard him with suspicion.

I have seven new joys. Want to hear them?

CAL: Not particularly.

WEI: First joy – new, glowing egg. Small, but steady. Second joy –

MARIANNE: If you please, Wei –

WEI: No trouble at all. Second joy – I'm much more respected now.

SLAVA: Not by us.

WEI: By everyone. Third joy…everyone wants to know me.

Indicating his glowing egg.

They want to know about this. Fourth joy…I forget the fourth joy. Forget the fifth joy, too…

HENRY: Dear God…

WEI: *Sixth* joy – no new members. I'm the last one in.

CAL: So everyone signed the agreement?

WEI: Yes. Nearly everyone. Seventh joy –

SLAVA: Who didn't sign?

HENRY: Yes, who?

WEI: Just some Asians. Seventh joy –

CAL: Which ones?

WEI: North Korea – you remember him, you got into that fight in the kitchen?

CAL: Oh, yeah. You fired him, right?

WEI: Not quite. Also India and Pakistan – I try to schedule them on different shifts. Also Israel is acting funny. No one really knows what they're doing. And *oh!* I forgot.

Pulling a small, glowing egg from his pocket.

South Africa is now a member!

Everyone groans. Suddenly the egg stops glowing.

Oops! Second thoughts, I guess.

SLAVA: *(As WEI stuffs the egg back in his pocket.)* I'm worried about this. Why don't these countries sign? Too many upstarts.

WEI: Maybe they would sign if you and Cal reduced a little.

CAL: *Reduced!?*

SLAVA: Are you crazy?

WEI: In the spirit of compromise?

They consider this.

CAL: It *is* costing us an arm and a leg.

SLAVA: And the other leg.

CAL: *(Of the goose egg-sized eggs.)* We wouldn't have to cut back to these levels. We could still be, you know, bigger.

SLAVA: Definitely bigger.

CAL: I'll give it a try if you will.

SLAVA: I don't know. It's very…sane.

CAL: I'm sure chaotic factors will appear no matter what.

SLAVA: True… All right. Let's reduce.

The others spontaneously – and genteelly – applaud.

CAL: But everybody else better cooperate, damn it. Let's get the rest of those Asians on board. No new members. Right?

SLAVA: *Da.*

MARIANNE: But of course.

HENRY: Without question.

They all look at WEI, who smiles broadly.

WEI: Seventh joy – the future!

WEI rises, picks up the two glowing, ostrich egg-sized eggs, and exits with them. SLAVA and CAL pull new eggs out of their pockets. These are not as big, but still noticeably larger than the other eggs on the table.

CAL: Now, that's a sacrifice.

SLAVA: A big one.

CAL: You know what that is there? That is statesmanship.

SLAVA: Absolutely. We are much more respectable now.

HENRY: I'd say so.

MARIANNE: *Certainment.*

CAL: I see a way forward now.

SLAVA: So do I.

WEI returns with a glowing goose egg-sized egg and a smaller table. He sets the smaller table down in front of the other table and puts the new egg on it.

MARIANNE: What is that?

WEI: Israel.

SLAVA: What?!

CAL: You're joking. When did *this* happen?

WEI: No one really knows. Don't worry, though; it's unofficial.

HENRY: Will the shock wave be unofficial also?

WEI: Probably not. Oh – and forgot about this.

Putting another glowing egg the same size as Israel's on the smaller table.

India, I'm afraid.

CAL: *India?!* We *gave* them stuff.

As the others look at him.

For…peaceful things, you know? For peace. You didn't help them, did you Wei?

WEI: Me? I hate them. They're rivals. We fight all the time.

SLAVA: He's got a point.

CAL: I'm really sorry about this. I had no clue they were… I had no clue.

SLAVA: Well, you'd better get one.

CAL: Look who's talking. You'd sell anything for the right price – assuming you can even keep track of it.

SLAVA: We've had a major downsizing! Things get lost!

HENRY: Gentlemen, gentlemen – please. We'll simply have to adjust, that's all. One more…small one shouldn't make all that much difference.

Suddenly angry shouts are heard from the kitchen. WEI exits.

MARIANNE: What's going on?

HENRY: I don't know.

The offstage hubbub increases: shouts, crashing sounds, things being thrown, etc.

CAL: Slava?

SLAVA: Don't ask me.

CAL: It's your wing!

The sounds suddenly stop. WEI re-enters.

WEI: It's nothing. One of the staff is Pakistani, and –

Pointing at the newest glowing egg.

He's a little miffed.

CAL: Miffed?!

WEI: How would you feel? India, his mortal enemy, has one of these. He's calmer now; I told him I'd help him.

MARIANNE: Help him what?

WEI: Get his own, of course.

The others all look at each other.

CAL: You can't do that.

WEI: Why not?

CAL: You signed the agreement!

WEI: *He* didn't.

HENRY: But you can't *help* him –

WEI: You helped India.

CAL: We didn't know we were helping them!

WEI: *(Skeptical.)* Really? In any case it created an intolerable imbalance of power. Pakistan must do something. When you think about it, it's a very reasonable request.

SLAVA: No, it isn't!

WEI: What do you know? You've left so many things lying around, these countries have almost no need of me. Don't tell me you're not making money on it. Besides –

Pulling another glowing egg from his pocket, the same size as the last one, and setting it on the smaller table.

It's already done. The Pakistani was very motivated.

CAL, SLAVA and HENRY all rise, outraged, speechless. Unperturbed, WEI sits.

MARIANNE: *(To WEI.)* Does this mean I can sell them a nuclear plant?

CAL: *No!* Well… I don't know. Probably not. Maybe.

MARIANNE: *(To WEI, making a 'phone-me' gesture.)* We'll talk.

HENRY: This is terrible. Pakistan is completely unreliable.

WEI: And you're such a model of restraint?

HENRY: Better than them!

WEI: And that's why you helped Iran build their nuclear program?

HENRY: That was years ago! Back under the Shah. We were *all* doing it!

CAL and MARIANNE look guilty.

WEI: You can't take back the knowledge.

HENRY: You're just sowing discord right now; that's all you're doing.

WEI: No, I'm being reasonable. When they have governments you like, you help them. When those governments disappear, and the technology you gave them remains, suddenly they're outlaws.

Indicating the glowing eggs.

I'm not the only reason more and more of these are showing up. I'm not even the main reason. Which reminds me –

WEI pulls out yet another small glowing egg and sets it on the table.

North Korea. He and the Pakistani are friends, it turns out. Apparently some money changed hands in exchange for…technology. Missiles went one way, nuclear weapons-making expertise went the other. Kind of a Silk Road thing, when you think about it. Been going on for centuries.

SLAVA: This is intolerable!

WEI: Why should you be the only ones with initiative? Now that I'm thinking of it –

WEI takes his own glowing egg off the table and replaces it with a slightly larger one.

MARIANNE: You're expanding?!

WEI: *(Polishing his new glowing egg vigorously.)* And modernizing. No point in having one of these if you don't test it.

MARIANNE: But we've all cut back.

HENRY: Been standing pat for years.

WEI: That's your business.

CAL: What part of the word 'agreement' don't you understand, Wei?

WEI: I am the only one of us to pledge never to use mine first. The only one! No first strike. Who among you has ever promised that? Who?!

CAL: It's only a promise, Wei.

SLAVA: Just words.

WEI: Then why don't you promise? What would it cost you? And speaking of 'just words'…

WEI pulls out a series of dove-sized glowing eggs – five in all – and sets them on the smaller table.

Belgium, Germany, Italy, Netherlands, Turkey.

CAL: They're not in the club!

WEI: NATO nuclear weapons sharing – deployed and stored in these nations. Their hands are on these weapons. Also Canada, South Korea and Greece for a time. Don't deny it; it was your idea.

CAL: We're still completely in charge of all those…those… things.

WEI: Really? What part of the word 'share' do you not understand? All of you try to control the flow of technology, but it's a losing game. Ultimately, every weapons system in history has become available to anyone who can pay for it or steal it. You constantly try to keep nuclear weapons out of your enemies' hands without ever asking why they have become your enemies. You are the cynics, not me.

MARIANNE: We're not cynics.

HENRY: We're just trying to survive.

SLAVA: Trying to help everyone survive.

CAL: Besides, nuclear weapons are raw power. No one can resist that. Their very existence *makes* people into enemies.

WEI: Nevertheless, trying to control them this way –

CAL: Would be a lot easier if you'd *help!*

WEI: First joy – ultimate power. Second joy – ultimate power has limits. Third joy – irony that forever attends the first two joys. Fourth joy – uncertainty: humanity's most steadfast companion. Fifth joy – I am growing richer than all of you, because I seek to control my*self*, not the rest of the world. Sixth joy – making friends out of enemies. Seventh joy –
But then, you all know the seventh joy.

THE OTHERS: *(Together, unenthusiastically.)* The future.

A knock at the front door.

WEI: Ooh. Sounds like a new applicant! I'd better get that.

WEI exits. The knock grows louder, and it is joined by other hands knocking, more and more until it's a rich and steady drumbeat at the door. Lights fade until only the glowing eggs are illuminated.

The End.

OPTION
by Amit Gupta

First production
The Tricycle Theatre, London, 9th February 2012

Characters / Cast

PRAKASH CHANDANA	Tariq Jordan
PROFESSOR SAEED AKRAM	Paul Bhattacharjee
DR. DIVYA MISHRA	Shereen Martin
Director	*Tara Robinson*

Setting
A laboratory in an Indian nuclear facility, 1968.

Lights fade up to reveal –

A laboratory in an Indian nuclear facility, 1968.

Sunrise visible through the back window.

Large room of someone senior – desks, workspaces – a coffee table with more informal chairs. A thermos sits on the coffee table as well as some cups.

A portrait of Mahatma Gandhi and a framed Indian flag on one wall. On another wall, a large blackboard in front of which stand two men:

PRAKASH CHANDANA, a physicist in his early twenties – boyish, enthusiastic, bright. He is scribbling a series of equations that we can't make out. He is focused and fast.

PROFESSOR SAEED AKRAM, a physicist in his sixties – watches the blackboard intently as PRAKASH writes. AKRAM refers to a notebook in his hand every so often, before looking back up at the blackboard.

PRAKASH: *(Referring to the blackboard.)* Here and here.

PRAKASH draws a line and stops.

PRAKASH: You see now Professor?

AKRAM: Yes.

AKRAM refers to the notebook.

AKRAM: There are some jumps here I didn't follow.

PRAKASH: I'm sorry, I got carried away. I've spent some time thinking around this... I simply wrote, I didn't...

AKRAM: Yes, I see that.

PRAKASH: In theory, an adjustment and we can...

AKRAM: *(Nodding.)* Yes, yes.

AKRAM looks through the notebook, mesmerised. After a while –

PRAKASH: It might save time by speeding up the process...in the reactor, speeding up everything...you know. *(Beat.)*

In theory at least.

AKRAM: In theory, yes.

PRAKASH: And the cost it might save…a simple adjustment only, if it works. *(Beat.)* The formulae work, my research supports it… I had thought there might be a way…small variation in the water, no more.

AKRAM looks back up at the blackboard.

PRAKASH: Professor? *(Beat.)* Professor?

AKRAM: Yes.

PRAKASH: What do you think?

Pause. The PROFESSOR looks at PRAKASH – then paces upstage and stops.

AKRAM: I think you should look out of the window.

PRAKASH: The window? *(Beat.)* Is that a metaphor for…

AKRAM: No, no. No metaphor. Just look out of the window *(Gesturing to the window at the back.) this* window.

PRAKASH: *That* window. Why?

AKRAM: Because I'm asking you to.

PRAKASH: Alright.

PRAKASH moves to the window, looks out carefully.

AKRAM: What do you see?

PRAKASH: I don't see anything.

AKRAM: Surely you see *something*.

PRAKASH: I see a few cars, some men sweeping, some *chowkidars.*

Pause.

AKRAM: Do you see the sky Prakash?

PRAKASH: The sky? Yes of course.

AKRAM: And yet you didn't mention it.

PRAKASH looks annoyed, like he's failed a test.

PRAKASH: No, I didn't.

AKRAM: How do you find it?

PRAKASH looks confused.

PRAKASH: I'm sorry? How do I find it?

AKRAM: It's not a trick question Prakash. There is no right or wrong answer. The sunrise. Describe it for me.

PRAKASH: *(Very methodically.)* Alright. Orange sky with some red, still…20, 22 per cent maybe…some blue lines but getting lighter, I'd say around 18 per cent of the sun now visible. Same as every morning.

AKRAM: That's very…precise. But do you see it every morning?

PRAKASH: Yes… Well, I mean, I see it I'm sure… I'm aware of it.

AKRAM: But you don't consciously look at it?

PRAKASH: No.

AKRAM: Because if you did, you'd know that every single sunrise is different.

PRAKASH: Yes, of course. I mean, of course, I know that to be true.

AKRAM: Good.

PRAKASH: But Professor, what did you think about my paper?

AKRAM: What I think, is that maybe you don't need to ask me what I think anymore. My former student is now teaching me things I didn't dream of.

PRAKASH: Professor. I remain your student always, without question, without hesitation. Without you…

AKRAM: You wouldn't have to fill in the gaps for an old man!

PRAKASH: Aren't the gaps where we sometimes find the light Professor? Didn't you say that?

AKRAM: Yes, I believe I did. And without light…

PRAKASH: There is only darkness.

Pause.

AKRAM: Prakash I didn't ask you to come in to discuss your paper. And to be clear, I didn't think you were wrong, not for a moment. There is not a single reason why it wouldn't work in practice. Its simplicity and elegance are quite astonishing to me. I couldn't see some of the steps, that's all.

I like to see the connections, the proof. Especially with my addled brain!

PRAKASH: I'm sorry, I should really take more care.

AKRAM: Don't apologise for your genius Prakash. Thank God for it. Yours or mine.

PRAKASH: Please professor.

AKRAM: Whatever you want to call it – your aptitude for original thought, your talent – it is a gift and I'm grateful it is yours, because such gifts should be exercised with humility and never brandished like a weapon.

Pause.

AKRAM: I think we need some more tea Prakash, don't you?

AKRAM removes the lid of the thermos flask on the coffee table and pours two cups. As he hands one to PRAKASH –

PRAKASH: Thank you.

PRAKASH takes a sip –

PRAKASH: Professor, if we didn't come in to discuss my paper, why did we come in so early?

AKRAM: I rather thought we'd watch *this* sunrise together, drink my wife's masala chai and talk.

PRAKASH: Oh, I see. May I ask why?

AKRAM: *Why?* I thought you like my wife's chai.

PRAKASH: I do. I mean, why today?

AKRAM: At certain times one has to step back and take in the world around us. And the autumn light is something we should never take for granted.

Beat.

Prakash, did you know that the word 'scientist' dates only to 1834. Do you know what we were called before then?

PRAKASH: No, what?

AKRAM: We were known as natural philosophers.

PRAKASH: I didn't know that.

AKRAM: It's a term I prefer because requires us to engage philosophically with everything around us. It also requires that certain questions remain at the forefront of our minds.

PRAKASH: What questions?

AKRAM: What is it you love most about what you do? Is it in harmony with your life as a whole?

PRAKASH: You want me to tell you?

AKRAM: Only if you want to.

Pause.

PRAKASH: What I love most about what I do is very simple.

It's the fact that what we know is only really what we once didn't know plus imagination. Which is what makes the unknown so exciting, the possibility of knowing.

We apply our minds, imagine the possibility, it becomes reality.

AKRAM: What if what you imagine is quite terrifying?

PRAKASH: For me, the possibility is always exciting. In fact, more so if it's terrifying, because it demands another solution.

AKRAM: I suppose you would feel that.

PRAKASH: And…

AKRAM: Yes?

PRAKASH: It is completely in harmony, because my work, this work, is my life. I don't need or want anything else.

AKRAM: One day that will change. When you marry, have children…

PRAKASH: There is some time left before then.

AKRAM: What time is it now?

PRAKASH: I don't know.

AKRAM: What happened to your watch?

PRAKASH: I'm not comfortable wearing it, it's too valuable, I might damage it.

AKRAM: I gave it to you, so you would wear it.

PRAKASH: But *you* don't wear a watch Professor?

AKRAM: That's why I like everyone else to!

PRAKASH: You could just wind up the clock on the wall.

AKRAM: But then it would just be a clock and have no meaning.

PRAKASH goes to the door.

AKRAM: *(Referring to the clock.)* One day, when I'm finished here, I'll explain.

PRAKASH goes out – comes back in a few moments later.

PRAKASH: It's six thirty-five.

AKRAM nods seriously.

AKRAM: Prakash, will you wipe the blackboard clean please?

PRAKASH: Of course.

PRAKASH wipes the blackboard, When he finishes –

PRAKASH: Professor, is something going on I should know about?

AKRAM: Yes. Any time now Dr. Mishra will arrive to see me. The conversation we will probably have is one I believe you should be party to.

PRAKASH: I didn't know Dr. Mishra was due back. Does she know I'll be here?

AKRAM: No. *(Beat.)* And I have something to ask, which I hope will not make you uncomfortable.

PRAKASH: Yes?

AKRAM: I'd prefer us not mention your paper. At least not for now.

PRAKASH: I can't see why it would come up…unless she asked me directly about it.

AKRAM: I don't want you to lie, I would never ask you to do that. Just not to bring it up.

PRAKASH: Of course.

Pause.

PRAKASH: What is Dr. Mishra coming to see you about?

AKRAM: Along with being Co-Director of this facility, she is now the chief atomic advisor to the government. In that capacity she has been attending some high-level talks and is now on her way here.

PRAKASH looks worried – AKRAM gets up and paces uncomfortably – looks out of the window again.

AKRAM: No need to look so worried.

PRAKASH: I'm not.

AKRAM: You know Prakash, Dr. Mishra was my brightest student. Until you.

The door opens. Enter DR. DIVYA MISHRA – in her late thirties/ early forties – she looks serious.

AKRAM: Divya.

DIVYA: Professor, when were… *(Seeing PRAKASH.)* Prakash, what are you doing here?

PRAKASH: The Professor asked me to come in.

DIVYA looks annoyed.

AKRAM: And I thought he should be here. *(Beat.)* Whereas I'm almost the past and you're very much the present, Prakash is our future!

Silence.

AKRAM: *(To DIVYA.)* Would you like some *chai*?

DIVYA: No. Thank you.

AKRAM: My wife's chai?

DIVYA: I'm fine.

Pause. DIVYA remains standing.

AKRAM: You're not going to sit down?

DIVYA looks at Prakash, then back at AKRAM.

DIVYA: I think it would be better if we discuss this on our own Professor.

PRAKASH looks uncomfortable and stands. He doesn't know what to do.

AKRAM: I would like him to stay.

DIVYA: I don't think it's a good idea.

Pause.

DIVYA: Alright. If this is what you want and you're happy for him to hear this.

AKRAM: I am.

DIVYA: Prakash, stay, please.

PRAKASH sits down. Silence.

AKRAM: So was I right?

DIVYA: Professor, when were you planning to tell me that your letter to the Minister was different to the one we discussed and agreed?

AKRAM: He opened it in front of you.

DIVYA: I gave it to him. He wanted to respond immediately.

Silence.

AKRAM: *(Matter of fact, not that sorry.)* I didn't have a chance to talk to you about the changes Divya. I should have thought.

Pause.

DIVYA: The Americans said no. They have refused to give us a nuclear security guarantee.

AKRAM: And our response?

DIVYA: The government will not sign the Non-Proliferation Treaty.

AKRAM shakes his head.

DIVYA: You didn't think the Americans would give us what
we asked for, but you thought our government would sign
anyway?

AKRAM: I was hoping that somebody would see sense.

DIVYA: The Soviets, the British, the French, now the
Americans.
They don't want anyone else to develop nuclear weapons,
but won't guarantee anyone's security against their use and
we're supposed to see sense?

AKRAM: It may be hypocritical.

DIVYA: It is hypocritcal.

AKRAM: Yes. But it is *not* surprising. You knew this was likely,
the government knew…

DIVYA: No. I thought it possible, not likely. I thought they
were open to discussing it again – that was the impression
they gave us. Then they asked why India needs such
a guarantee when the UN is already our security. The
Minister pointed out that China sits on the Security
Council, so has the right of veto, which means…

AKRAM: Yes, I know what it means.

Pause. DIVYA looks upset.

AKRAM: Divya, sit down. *(Beat.)* Please.

DIVYA sits down. AKRAM pours a cup of chai – hands it to her.

AKRAM: I'm sorry I didn't talk to you about the letter.
Especially since you delivered it.

DIVYA nods. Silence.

PRAKASH: What does China's veto mean?

DIVYA: It means they could support Pakistan in a war, threaten
us, attack, and if they claim provocation, veto UN action to
support us.

PRAKASH: Even if we didn't start it?

DIVYA: Yes.

PRAKASH: Then that means the UN is…

DIVYA: …powerless.

PRAKASH: So we've been trying to get a security guarantee from one of the nuclear powers.

DIVYA: Yes. *(Beat.)* In turn, we would sign the Non-Proliferation Treaty and commit to not pursuing a nuclear weapons option.

Pause.

AKRAM: The truth is our government have been naive in believing the new President, Mr. Nixon, would be any different. He wants his country out of Vietnam, so will never risk upsetting the Chinese. The talks were doomed to fail from the start.

DIVYA: Was it naive to think that a new regime might see the position we're being forced into.

AKRAM: Nobody is being forced into anything! Politicians will always say this and it's not true.

DIVYA: Isn't it? *(Turns to PRAKASH.)* What does it sound like to you Prakash?

Before PRAKASH can answer.

AKRAM: The government's agenda is not ours.

DIVYA: May I ask then, what is our agenda now?

AKRAM: You need to ask me that?

DIVYA: Yes. And maybe it's good that Prakash should also hear this.

Pause.

AKRAM: Our agenda is exactly the same as it has been since independence. Since the Department of Atomic Energy was created. Nuclear research to provide India with the power to make her self sufficient. Use of the atom for civil purposes only.

DIVYA: But now how can security not be *our* agenda too? After independence our situation with the Chinese was completely different. We had, at least, an understanding.

AKRAM: You want to talk about our security Divya? Have you changed your mind?

DIVYA: You didn't get a chance to talk me about your letter to the Minister, so I'd just like to know that whatever course of action *we* choose, we have talked through together and are clear about all of the consequences.

Pause.

AKRAM: Alright. Let us talk about our security.

DIVYA: Good.

AKRAM: You still agree our primary strategic concern is China? That Pakistan, given the current strength of our conventional forces, is a manageable threat?

DIVYA: Yes.

AKRAM: Prakash, what do you think?

PRAKASH: Yes, from what I understand.

AKRAM: Good. Because China's nuclear status is nothing to do with us. It is only about posturing and prestige – it has more to do with the US and Soviets than it does with us. China does not represent a nuclear threat. Their military threat remains conventional, and our army is now more than strong enough to contain that.

DIVYA: But three years ago, before the war with Pakistan…

AKRAM nods but says nothing – DIVYA turns to PRAKASH.

PRAKASH: They threatened to attack us.

DIVYA: Across the Himalayas. They promised 'grave consequences' if we went to war with Pakistan. What do you think they meant by that exactly?

AKRAM: *(Irritated.)* Does it matter what they meant? We went to war with Pakistan and *nothing* happened.

DIVYA: How do we know that nothing will happen in the future?

AKRAM: *Something* will always happen, but what you and I both do know is that a nuclear test explosion is some considerable distance from an effective weapon!

DIVYA: They have bombs. A number now.

AKRAM: Could their aircraft even get into Indian airspace to drop them without being shot down first?

DIVYA: We can't know, which means there's a chance of one getting through. Can we take that chance? Should we?

Silence.

DIVYA: We had an agreement. We said we would choose our course of action together.

AKRAM: Yes. But I realised that the only way to be taken seriously was not to threaten, but to actually resign.

PRAKASH: You've resigned Professor?

AKRAM looks at PRAKASH. He's about to say something, when he turns back to DIVYA.

AKRAM: Yes. At least I have offered my resignation, conditional upon… *(To DIVYA.)* What was the Minister's response?

DIVYA: He has not accepted it yet. He asked me to make clear that our not signing the Treaty does not necessarily mean pursuing a new course.

AKRAM: But to be clear, not signing does mean that we have now for the first time, officially adopted a nuclear weapons *option*, does it not?

DIVYA: An option, yes.

AKRAM: And an option makes having that particular option inevitable don't you think?

DIVYA: No I don't. I don't think that.

AKRAM: Even given the number of hawks who are pressing for us to develop nuclear weapons?

DIVYA: But isn't that a stronger reason to stay, Professor? To be the steadying voices in the room. It has worked for the last four years.

AKRAM: Until today we hadn't committed to a nuclear weapons *option*.

Pause.

DIVYA: The Minister wants you to reconsider.

AKRAM: And he asked you to...

DIVYA: Talk it through with you.

Pause.

AKRAM: Alright Divya.

DIVYA: Thank you. *(Beat.)*

As of today the US are imposing sanctions and have cut aid.

AKRAM: And our old friends the Soviets are now funding Pakistan. So what do we have to lose from anyone? It frees us to make choices based on what is right for India, not on who we do not want to upset.

DIVYA: We've always had foreign assistance for our Nuclear Programme. And access will now be restricted. Other countries will be pressured into not assisting us.

AKRAM: So it's more important than ever for scientists like us to stay on the ship, whatever the course. Is that it, is that what they're saying?

DIVYA: If you want to put it like that, yes.

AKRAM: But don't you see, if we have no foreign assistance, resigning could very well force the government to reconsider?

DIVYA: I haven't resigned Professor. Your resignation has not yet been accepted. And *we* agreed on an ultimatum. Six months and see what changed in the event the NPT was not signed.
We agreed.

AKRAM: Yes. We did. But I believe we were wrong. And I am certain the government, if pressured, will reconsider.

DIVYA: The government will not reconsider and will not sign the Treaty. The Minister has made that absolutely clear, the cabinet are unanimous.

AKRAM: How would they replace us? Who would they replace us with?

DIVYA: There are many who will support the government's decision.

AKRAM: *(Resolutely.)* But if enough of us stop, they *will* have to think again!

DIVYA: *(Shaking her head.)* All it will do is slow down everything we've been working on. That's all that will be achieved.

Silence.

PRAKASH: Professor?

AKRAM: Yes?

PRAKASH: Our work? What happens to it if... Would we really just abandon it?

AKRAM: They're leaving me with no alternative. *(Quietly to PRAKASH.)* 'If it's not in harmony with your life as a whole' Prakash...

PRAKASH: Is there really no other way?

Silence.

DIVYA: There is an alternative, Professor.

AKRAM shakes his head.

PRAKASH: What alternative? *(Beat.)* Professor, is it not worth trying everything to find a solution? Is it not worth hearing out?

AKRAM: Alright. *(Beat.)* Divya?

DIVYA: We finish the work that's been started. On the new reactors, which are purely for civil use – work that will be very hard to complete quickly if we leave and will leave millions of Indians without the possibility of power for the rest of their lives. We finish that. Which will take a year, a year and a half...

AKRAM: We'd agreed six months. Now you're talking about a year and a half?

DIVYA: Maybe it will take less time. Any breakthrough could speed everything up. Then we see what the government does. If nothing changes...

AKRAM: But don't you see, it already has. Yesterday we were a nation who were committed to nuclear weapons disarmament, today we are a nation with a nuclear weapons option!

AKRAM shakes his head, gets up and walks to the window.

AKRAM: These last twenty years we've built up a considerable nuclear infrastructure from nothing. *(Beat.)* From the beginning we had a Prime Minister who was clear about what India meant to Indians, so there was never a doubt that our work contradicted our own beliefs or were ever contrary to Gandhi-*ji's* philosophy of peace, non-violence.

Without those teachings, would there even be an India now? And protecting his philosophy has always been at the heart of how we live as Indians.

Beat.

So when Pandit Nehru pressed for total international nuclear weapon disarmament, it was completely consistent with everything we stood for. And when he then founded the Non-Alignment Movement, India's identity was clear and unambiguous to the world also. We would not ally with the Soviet Union or the United States, whatever that meant economically, because it was against our principles.

And India was seen as a leader, as an example to be followed.

Beat.

Even when we knew the policy China was pursuing, we stayed true to our own course and were admired for it.

So when I see us turning our backs on who we are and what we represent as a nation, it's something I don't feel I can ever be part of, or ever understand, because it's not who we are. *(To PRAKASH.)* You understand, don't you?

PRAKASH nods.

PRAKASH: Yes.

AKRAM: Divya? You know this.

DIVYA: Yes I do. But what if the way of holding on to who we are as a nation now means compromise, because things have changed so much.

You remember what most people were demanding after China's test? They wanted us to have our own bomb. The newspapers all pressed for this…

AKRAM: Out of fear, not out of knowledge.

DIVYA: The same with the politicians. A majority of Congress, the party of Nehru, wanted the bomb.

AKRAM: Yes, and you remember what Prime Minister Shastri said?

He called the Chinese test a danger to the maintenance of peace but three days later reaffirmed that Indian nuclear policy would remain unchanged. We, the India of Nehru and Gandhi, would not emulate the Chinese, we would not develop and test nuclear bombs!

And the world admired him for taking that stance.

Pause.

PRAKASH: Professor, may I ask a question?

AKRAM: Of course, Prakash.

PRAKASH: Why should anyone else decide what's right for us?

AKRAM: That's precisely what I'm saying. We fulfil our own destiny. Our destiny is based on our founding principles.

PRAKASH: No, I mean, why shouldn't we develop a nuclear bomb?

AKRAM looks shocked.

AKRAM: Prakash? Have you been listening to anything I said?

PRAKASH: Of course, I mean no disrespect, what I'm saying is…

Just, the option to have nuclear weapons to deter others from using them – surely that *can* be reconciled with Gandhi-*ji's* teachings?

Isn't it what we *don't* do with them that shows who we are as a nation. If it makes others more cautious, if it promotes peace? And that would mean we could carry on with our work.

AKRAM: So would you have us spend billions of rupees, compromise our social and economic development programmes for decades to come, to develop weapons that we never intend to use?

PRAKASH: I don't know, I don't think I was saying that, I just...

DIVYA: Spending huge sums of money is not being proposed.

AKRAM: Then tell me what is?

DIVYA: Continuing our atomic strategy as is. *(Beat.)* And, if necessary, increase our research and development resources in nuclear explosion technology, with the possible option of creating and demonstrating a PNE – a peaceful nuclear explosion.

AKRAM: *(Shocked.)* A peaceful nuclear explosion?

DIVYA: It would be an extension of the work we are doing already. The technology would be appropriate for our atomic energy programme...

AKRAM: But people would think that we had a bomb, is that right?

DIVYA: We wouldn't have a bomb.

AKRAM: We'd have the technology.

DIVYA: They would know that we could create a nuclear explosion – which in itself would be a deterrent!

AKRAM: *(Angry.)* Creating fear should never be a deterrent!

Beat.

But I see, it makes perfect sense to me now. The country that gained its independence through peaceful means – the nation of the *Mahatma* – adapts her own philosophy to show the world how a nuclear explosion can be completely peaceful, rather than a trigger to set off an arms race with Pakistan – a nation who are our own brothers!

Silence.

DIVYA turns to PRAKASH.

DIVYA: Would you step out for a moment please?

AKRAM: Whatever you want to say, you can say in front of Prakash.

DIVYA: Just for a minute. Please.

PRAKASH nods and steps out of the room.

DIVYA: Professor, there's something I feel uncomfortable telling you, but feel you should know. Before you hear it from someone else.

AKRAM: What is it?

DIVYA: The Minister said that there had been serious questions about your ability to not feel personally conflicted.

AKRAM: Because like the founder of our nation I am a pacifist!

DIVYA: No, because you're Muslim and still have many relatives in Pakistan.

AKRAM: *(Shocked.)* What?

DIVYA: He said, there are people who have questioned your loyalty to India, because of your stance. The fact that you have referred on a number of occasions to Pakistanis as our brothers. They feel you're overly sympathetic to Pakistan.

AKRAM: They questioned my loyalty?

DIVYA: Yes.

AKRAM: He said that?

DIVYA: He did.

AKRAM: This is completely absurd, I helped create this Department? Nehru-*ji* was friend of mine, how can they say this?

DIVYA: I know, it hurts me to tell you this, but I feel you should know.

Pause.

AKRAM: So if I resign, they'll say I did this because I don't love my country?

DIVYA: No! The Minister was clear that he will not let that happen. He said he didn't expect you to change your mind, but wanted me to try to talk to you about it. But whatever you decided, we couldn't afford to lose anyone else. People who would follow. Like Prakash and Kumar, some of the others – if they were to follow, he may not be able to stop people from speculating, because of the potential damage to the Department.

Silence.

AKRAM: And they would be accused of being disloyal too? Traitors even? Have their careers completely ruined? Is that right?

DIVYA: I'm sorry Professor, when he told me this I was ready to resign also, but I thought I might be able to persuade you, make you see that as it stands now – the PNE, everything that goes with it – may not be necessary, if *we* stay here and lead the way. So I was hoping I wouldn't need to tell you any of this.

Silence.

DIVYA: Professor?

AKRAM: For me, ambiguity cannot exist in what we do. We go one way or another. The distinction in what we do has to be unequivocal – nuclear technology for peaceful means or for military. What it has to come down to is what we want to be as a nation? Who we want to be as a nation?

DIVYA: At the moment, a lot of people want a nation that is respected, perhaps even feared rather than admired.

AKRAM nods.

AKRAM: Yes, I see that now.

DIVYA: And I've seen at first hand what the choices are for the government. So you see I have to stay. And I hope you can understand that.

AKRAM nods, before going over to the door. He lets PRAKASH back in. before picking up his bag – moving over to a side table and starting to remove some of his possessions.

PRAKASH: Professor, are you really going to leave?

AKRAM: I have to.

Pause.

PRAKASH: *(Hesitant.)* If you think this is the right thing to do, Professor, I'll leave with you, of course, my loyalty is to you.

As soon as the others follow, we'll be able to get back to our work.

AKRAM: No.

PRAKASH: I'm sorry?

AKRAM: No. I don't want you to do that. I want you to stay.

PRAKASH: I don't understand. Why?

AKRAM: I may not agree with Dr. Mishra, but she might be right. And she will need you to help keep us on the right path – perhaps your paper may even speed up the process.

DIVYA: Professor, please, you don't have to do this.

AKRAM moves over to DIVYA, takes her hands –

AKRAM: You don't need me Divya and this is a journey I can never make.

Silence as AKRAM picks up his bag and goes over to the door.

AKRAM: Prakash?

PRAKASH: Yes?

AKRAM: *(Gesturing to the clock.)* The time on the clock?

PRAKASH: Yes.

AKRAM: It's the time my granddaughter was born. Nothing matters to me more than her. The world I would like her to live in remains my compass, always. Do you understand?

PRAKASH: Yes.

As AKRAM leaves.

Lights out.

LITTLE RUSSIANS
by John Donnelly

First production
The Tricycle Theatre, London, 9th February 2012

Characters / Cast

YURI	
20s, Ukrainian	Tariq Jordan
VLADIMIR	
50s, Russian army officer	Simon Rouse
ANDREI	
20s, Ukrainian	Rick Warden
IRINA	
40s, Ukrainian	Nathalie Armin
DENNIS	
30s, Chechen	Daniel Rabin
JOHNSON	
US Captain	Simon Chandler
CHECHEN HEAVY	Paul Bhattacharjee
RUSSIAN JUNIOR OFFICER	
or PRIVATE	Michael Cochrane
US PRIVATES	Shereen Martin
	David Yip
Director	*Nicolas Kent*

Accents

Accents here are *not* allegorical. Rather they are used as a kind of shorthand for cultural differences and relationships between nations. This – like much of what follows – is best taken with a pinch of salt.

Russians speak with a standard English accent.

Ukrainians speak with the accent of the Irish Republic (alternatively that of any UK nation other than England).

Chechens speak with a Turkish or Arabic accent.

Americans speak with an American accent.

Dennis and Johnson may be played by male or female actors.

Thanks to Vera Filatova and Jem Horner

A small woodland clearing by a lake in Central Ukraine.

An SS20 nuclear missile on its side set on a conflat on railway tracks. A ladder allows access to the top. Much of the outer casing has been stripped, as have the tracks – only the section immediately underneath the conflat remains.

1

Late Summer.

A Ukrainian flag. A nuclear missile with beer cans on top.

VLADIMIR, a uniformed but dishevelled medical officer in the Red Army; and YURI, who wears tracksuit bottoms and trainers with a makeshift Ukrainian army jacket worn over an FC Chornomorets Odessa shirt.

They are pointing guns at one another.

VLADIMIR: It's 1993

YURI: I know it is, what a weird thing to say. I mean if we're going to be stating obvious facts, why not just go the whole hog, y'know, here we are, two soldiers, you Russian, me Ukrainian, stood in some woods by a lake in the middle of the Ukraine, to be more specific, an area of the Ukraine that technically doesn't exist – that isn't actually on any maps because it's a militarised zone, talking about that nuclear missile there. I mean if I said all that, that would be weird wouldn't it?

VLADIMIR: What I mean is you're disarming

YURI: Thanks, you have a winning smile yourself

VLADIMIR: The Ukrainian government is disarming. That's why I'm here for the missile

YURI: Your lot can't be trusted to keep the phones and electric running, I'm hardly going to just hand over a nuclear missile on your say so

VLADIMIR: You run your own country now

YURI: All the more reason not to hand over nuclear warheads to some Eskimowhacking Russkie

VLADIMIR: What do you want it for, you don't even have the launch codes?

YURI: Scrap

VLADIMIR: You want a nuclear missile for scrap?

YURI: The metal casing, the parts, it's good metal. We already stripped most of it

VLADIMIR: There's uranium in there!

YURI: I used gloves

VLADIMIR: You know how much it's worth?

YURI: How much you offering?

VLADIMIR: We own it

YURI: It's on our land

VLADIMIR: You said this was a militarised zone

YURI: Ah sure, but no one comes here, not since ages anyway

VLADIMIR: I've been sent by the Kremlin

YURI: You hear that? That'll be my knees knocking with fear

VLADIMIR: It's a joint operation, the Americans and Russia working together, your government has instructed us to reclaim the missiles

YURI: On your own?

VLADIMIR: What?

YURI: You'll have trouble shifting it on your own, what you planning on, hoiking it on your shoulder?

VLADIMIR: My unit is on its way

YURI: Well, why don't we wait till your unit gets here?

ANDREI enters, pointing a rifle at VLADIMIR. He wears an Iron Maiden T-shirt.

ANDREI: Who's the Eskimowhacker?

VLADIMIR turns, trying to point his gun at ANDREI and YURI at the same time.

YURI: Ah, he wants the thing

VLADIMIR: You mean the missile?

ANDREI: Can it, ballbag, I'm talking to my brother. Of course the missile, what else would I mean?

VLADIMIR: Who's in charge?

ANDREI: I am

YURI: I'm the one with military training

ANDREI: Military training my arse. Even our shitehawk army wouldn't touch him, and they'll take any nutter

YURI: It's not my fault I've a club foot!

ANDREI: He got our mum to make him his own uniform with a needle and thread, how nutty is that?

YURI: I love my country

VLADIMIR: I confess it looks a tad unusual

YURI: Watch your mouth or you're getting it

VLADIMIR: Maybe it's time I left

ANDREI: Stop right there!

YURI: Don't be scared of him, he's never fired that thing in his life

ANDREI: Don't tell him that!

YURI: Why not, it's true

ANDREI: You don't tell him that though, Yuri, you idiot. If he thinks I won't shoot, we lose our leverage

YURI: What leverage?

ANDREI: Our bargaining power. At least if he thinks I'll shoot him we've got something to bargain with

YURI: But you won't shoot him

ANDREI: Yes, but he doesn't know that

YURI: Leverage, bargaining power, you sound like a Russian

VLADIMIR: He really won't fire that?

YURI: I will, drop your pea shooter

ANDREI: What's wrong with sounding Russian, anyhow? I hate this stinking country. All we do is complain about the Russians, it's our national pastime

YURI: There's a lot to complain about. They stole our entire country. You got upset enough when I stole your diary

ANDREI: A diary is personal!

YURI: 'Dear Diary, I have such dark thoughts'

ANDREI: You sound like an ignorant peasant

YURI: Well you sound like a bleating cow

ANDREI: Cows don't bleat you idiot! They moo! Moo! Moo!

YURI: They do so bleat, I've heard them. They mutated from drinking all the radiation water from Chernobyl

ANDREI: Chernobyl was a hundred miles away!

YURI: So how come Old Man Andropov who lives by the stream, how come his kids have noses next to their ears?

VLADIMIR is sneaking off.

ANDREI: Because Old Man Andropov married his own sister, just like everyone else in this half-bred town

YURI: Hey! Where you think you're going?

VLADIMIR: This is clearly a family matter, you have much to discuss

YURI: Your next move will be your last

VLADIMIR: I don't think so. After forty years in the Red Army, you get a sense for the kind of man who'll fire a gun and the kind who won't. You're the kind who won't

YURI shoots a beer can off the missile. VLADIMIR lets out a cry and drops his gun which YURI collects.

Stalin's teeth, that's a nuclear missile with the casing stripped! You'll kill us all!

YURI: Ooh! Health and safety!

We can't let him go, he'll tell his unit about the thing and the Russians and the Americans will come and steal our scrap

VLADIMIR: I won't tell a soul

YURI pulls a knife.

YURI: I vote we decapitate him, put his head on a spike

ANDREI: Why would we do that?

YURI: Send a message

ANDREI: What's the message? 'We are nutters'

VLADIMIR: Don't decapitate me, I haven't got a unit!

ANDREI: So why did you say you did?

YURI: Talk fast you son of a Muscovite pigdog!

VLADIMIR: I was attached to a unit searching for the missile

YURI: So you do have a unit

VLADIMIR: Was! Was! I'm medical corps. I fell ill, a little gout, nothing serious, and was discharged on health grounds

ANDREI: A doctor discharged on health grounds

VLADIMIR: And those rumours weren't true

ANDREI: What rumours?

VLADIMIR: Forty years I gave them. The killing fields of
Lithuania, the testing grounds of Kazakhstan, those
accursed months on the Black Sea with only Sergei and his
curious moonshine to dull the pain. How did they reward
me? By accusing me of being a raving dipsomaniac. Lies,
all lies. Not one single soul died while I was conscious.

ANDREI: How do you even know about the thing? The trains
used to shoot by at all hours, keeping us up, one day we
just woke to find it sat there

VLADIMIR: Before the Union fell, they would shuttle the
warheads all over the Empire, often in woodland to throw
off the spy planes. Now Yeltsin has joined the Americans
they want all the missiles in their control, but since the
fall...it's a bureaucrat's nightmare, the amount of lost
paperwork, Gorky himself wouldn't credit it. There's task
forces looking for this. We know it left a location one
hundred miles East, heading West and it didn't arrive.
We figured we'd just follow the train tracks, but they keep
disappearing –

YURI: Train tracks, they're looking for train tracks!

VLADIMIR: What's so funny?

YURI: You think we're just going to leave good steel lying
around?

ANDREI: Few yards of track, a family can eat for weeks

VLADIMIR: The task force is combing the area, quadrant by
quadrant. It's a matter of time before they find it, but if we
can shift it before they get here, they'll be none the wiser

ANDREI: Shift it on to who?

VLADIMIR: Taliban, Chechens, where there's a power vacuum, there's a market

ANDREI: You have contacts?

VLADIMIR: From my Black Sea days. If truth be told, that's why I left my unit, I was going to sell the warheads. *We* can sell the warheads, we can be rich

ANDREI takes YURI aside.

ANDREI: He worked in the testing grounds, he was on the Black Sea for god's sake, you know what those guys are like

YURI: I still say we kill him

ANDREI: We can't kill him, we're civilised human beings

YURI: Speak for yourself, I've been brutalised by years of Soviet oppression.

ANDREI: How do we know you're not just buying time till your comrades get here?

VLADIMIR: Why would I tell the Russians and the Americans? I tell them I get nothing. It goes straight to the government.

YURI: I still say we're better off using it for scrap

ANDREI: *(To VLADIMIR.)* How much are they worth these missiles?

VLADIMIR: In this state, to us, a few million US dollars

YURI: What do I need US dollars for?

ANDREI: Always thinking like a peasant. Think big. Think Russian.

YURI: I don't want to think Russian

ANDREI: Fine! Think American then. They hate the Eskimowhackers as much as you do

YURI: Then how come they're working together to get the thing

ANDREI: Because they don't want the Ukraine to have a missile. They think we can't be trusted with it. Think of this as one in the eye of the motherland, a blow to the people who drove our proud Ukrainian father to an early grave. This is your chance to do something for your country

VLADIMIR: And get rich in the process

ANDREI: Do it for papa, Yuri

YURI: No funny business

VLADIMIR: We'll split the money, three ways

YURI: No way, we do this, we get sixty you get forty

VLADIMIR: Done

ANDREI: Hang on, no deal. Yuri, you grebo, sixty forty, that's worse than three ways.

(To VLADIMIR.) We get eighty-five you get fifteen

VLADIMIR: Eighty twenty

ANDREI: Done

VLADIMIR: Like a suckling pig on a spit

YURI: Are you sure that's better than three ways?

Enter IRINA.

IRINA: Oh hello

VLADIMIR: And who is this?

IRINA: Aren't you going to introduce me?

ANDREI: Mother, we are in the middle of important negotiations

VLADIMIR: Mother? To these boys, surely not! You must have had them very young

IRINA: I was a precocious child

VLADIMIR: Doctor Vladimir Mihailovich, Red Army, medical corps

IRINA: And will the good doctor be spending the night with me, I mean with us?

YURI: He's not staying in the house

ANDREI: He can have the fishing hut by the lake, Yuri will show you down

VLADIMIR kisses her hand.

VLADIMIR: I am in your debt, Madam

IRINA: I'll fetch you down a little something later. You look ravishing, I mean ravished, I mean famished

YURI: Come on.

YURI leads VLADIMIR off.

2

Night time.

IRINA and VLADIMIR sit on top of the missile.

VLADIMIR eats dumplings, greedily.

IRINA: Andrei was always the entrepreneur. He has dreams of hosting a rave in a nuclear reactor. Yuri's the hands on one, he's a whiz with anything electronic. He even wired us up so we get American television. MTV, CNN. *Baywatch* is his favourite. He's training to be a lifeguard

VLADIMIR: There's plenty of call on the Black Sea coast

IRINA: I often hear him in his room practising his stroke. Don't mind my boys, Vladimir. They may come over like psychopathic cattle botherers but their hearts are in the right place. Since their father died, god rest his soul, I've done my best, but there are some needs only a man can fulfil

VLADIMIR: You never thought of remarrying?

IRINA: Who'd have me?

VLADIMIR continues to eat, oblivious to the offer. IRINA rolls her eyes.

Is there a Madam Doctor Mihailovich?

VLADIMIR: I've never had much luck with women

IRINA: Strange. A handsome soldier like yourself, a medical man to boot, with your intellect, your charm and your prospects... Do you have prospects?

VLADIMIR: I have my army pension to look forward to

IRINA: I suppose an army pension isn't as much as they say

VLADIMIR: There are extras

IRINA: Extras?

VLADIMIR: *(Taps his nose.)* Extras

IRINA: Ohh!

(Taps her nose.) Extras!

No, you've lost me, what are they?

VLADIMIR: The black market

IRINA: Any dependents, invalid aunts, an idiot love child perhaps?

VLADIMIR: Not to my certain knowledge

IRINA: I'll bet you've seen sights that would make a woman blush

VLADIMIR: Or a cabin boy's eyes mist over

IRINA: Sorry?

VLADIMIR: Nothing fit for your beautiful ears, my dear

IRINA: Nothing that passes your lips could shock me

VLADIMIR: I remember the sheep at Semipalatinsk

IRINA: Right, this may be the country, but there are limits

VLADIMIR: They test the bombs there. It's a Kazakh military site, not dissimilar to here in fact. They keep cattle in the pens at one hundred metre intervals from the blast, towers filled with pigs, sheep, goats, cows – at various levels. They detonate the bombs then see the effect at different distances and heights

IRINA: Must put them off their feed

VLADIMIR: One time I went in a few days after the blast – first few pens, nothing survives, charred beyond recognition. Then after a few hundred metres, limbs, heads, hooves. Further still, mutilated corpses, a goat's severed head had landed by a decapitated pig, like the imaginings of some deranged scientist –

IRINA: Keep it light

VLADIMIR: – further out, animals with their flesh seared off but still breathing –

IRINA: More dumplings?

VLADIMIR: – a lamb, silver with the ash, tripping blindly in circles. They say the blast is like staring at the sun. Opened its mouth to cry for its mother but no noise. Little orphan lamb

IRINA: I too have suffered at the hands of men

VLADIMIR: I can't imagine

IRINA: Try

VLADIMIR: Let me care for you, Irina

IRINA: Vladi! Surely you're not suggesting taking up with me, living off the army pension you'd have wired here, subsidised by your black market earnings?

VLADIMIR: I know I'm old but I have ten good years left in me

IRINA: That many?

VLADIMIR: Unless some terrible accident befalls me

IRINA: Let's not dwell on such things

VLADIMIR: You're right

IRINA: The thought of your death fills my heart with sorrow too great to mention. Do you have a will?

VLADIMIR: A will?

IRINA: I couldn't bear the thought of your pension and *(Taps her nose.)* extras falling into the wrong hands. I could be your faithful executioner, I mean executor

VLADIMIR: I'm a mad old fool, Irina

IRINA: You are

VLADIMIR: Flower of the Ukraine!

IRINA: My boys mentioned you have contacts

VLADIMIR: Oh yes, your little ornament

IRINA: Hardly little!

VLADIMIR: It's strange, it feels smaller when you're sat astride it

IRINA: I know that feeling

VLADIMIR: Through my days in the Black Sea Fleet, well, I do have...contacts

IRINA: May I speak frankly

VLADIMIR: I'd prefer it if you did

IRINA: My boys know little of the world. It might be best if you deal with me

VLADIMIR: Sweet woman, I could never betray them, I gave them my word

IRINA: What are they offering you?

VLADIMIR: Seventy-thirty in their favour

IRINA: What if I were to offer you sixty-forty instead?

VLADIMIR: Done

3

A home-made Russian flag has usurped the Ukrainian standard.

ANDREI shoots beer cans off the missile. Sometimes a beer can flies off. Sometimes we hear the bullet ricochet off the missile. Occasionally, we hear sex noises from off.

YURI enters, carrying a radio. He sets about fixing it.

ANDREI: Our own mother!

YURI: Is there no decency?

ANDREI: There we were with a perfectly above board deal to sell a nuclear warhead on the black market and she sells us down the river

YURI: You can't trust anyone these days

ANDREI: I'm not sure the old days were better, Yuri.

   (Calling out.) Are you done yet?

IRINA: *(Calling from offstage.)* Nearly there!

ANDREI: I mean granted, after the collapse of the Soviet Union the oligarchs exploited the power vacuum, which, when aligned to Western capitalism resulted in the terror of hyperinflation and the black market, but look on the bright side – at least these days you're not tortured for writing poetry

YURI: I couldn't make head nor tail of that dissident poetry

ANDREI: Sure, that's the point of poetry

YURI: This international arms dealing business, it's more stressful than you think

ANDREI: D'you know I was thinking the same thing? Compared to lugging scrap around, I thought it'd be a walk in the park, but it's really quite taxing, you know it weighs heavy on your conscience

YURI: Do you think we can trust these Chechens your man says he can sell it to?

ANDREI: Once you dig beneath the superficial weapons of mass destruction business, I'm sure deep down these are just honest fellas making a living

YURI: I'm not sure I trust the Russian

ANDREI: I can't be having your anti-Russian guff Yuri, the man's got a contact

YURI: Contact my arse. He's landed a cushy deal with mother, he's got his oats in both senses. It's been a month now

ANDREI: Yuri, he's selling a nuclear fecking missile not flogging a clapped out Trabant down the market, he's got to get the messages through, arrange the meetings and that, these things take time

YURI: We haven't got time. The task force, the Russians and the Yanks, they're on to us

ANDREI: How do you know?

YURI: I fixed up the radio receiver. The signal's not great but late at night I hear the spies talking in code

ANDREI: What kind of code?

YURI: There's one phrase in particular. You'll hear this really weird sound like, then this voice will come on and say, 'That's so good I'll play it again'.

ANDREI: Can you make anything else out?

YURI: Only one other phrase

ANDREI: Which is?

YURI: The John Peel Show

ANDREI: That does sound strange

YURI: We've got to do something, or the Russians and Americans will take the thing and we'll get nothing, not even scrap

ANDREI: So what would you suggest then? What's your bright idea

YURI: We don't need Vladimir

ANDREI: He's the one with the contact

YURI: Maybe he's not the only one

ANDREI: What do you mean?

YURI: Maybe I've found my own contact

ANDREI: You found a contact to sell a nuclear missile?

YURI: Maybe

ANDREI: Where would you have found a contact for a nuclear missile?

YURI: Down the pub

ANDREI: Which pub?

YURI: It hasn't got a name

ANDREI: You found a contact for the thing in a pub that hasn't got a name? You're an idiot, Yuri

YURI: I'm the idiot? I'm not the one who wants to host a rave in a nuclear reactor

ANDREI: A disused nuclear reactor! How many times, they had to halt construction after Chernobyl, these concrete shells sat on the Black Sea, waiting to be used, like everything in this fecking country

YURI: At least in a nuclear reactor, you'll save money on the glowsticks

ANDREI: There's no radiation, you idiot. Don't mess this up, we need to stick with Vladimir

YURI: We haven't got time to wait

ANDREI: Yuri

YURI: Okay maybe I don't have a contact – yet, but I'll find one

ANDREI: I'm warning you Yuri, don't balls this up

YURI: I'll give you a couple of days. No more. Else I start pursuing my contact

ANDREI: You don't have a contact

YURI: I so do!

ANDREI: And stop getting on at mum all the time, otherwise she'll chuck us out on our ear

IRINA enters, a little dishevelled, wearing what appears to be a neckerchief.

IRINA: Boys, not arguing I hope

YURI: How's your Russian boyfriend?

IRINA: Be nice to your mother

ANDREI: *(Mouths.)* Go on

YURI: I like your scarf

IRINA: I'm not wearing a scarf. Oh goodness, my blindfold's fallen down

YURI: Oh mother, please!

IRINA: We're just playing hide and seek

ANDREI: Betraying us with that Eskimowhacker

IRINA: He loves me, he's always saying romantic things

YURI: Like what? What's the most romantic thing he's ever said?

IRINA: *(Thinks.)* 'Turn around'

ANDREI: Everything was fine till you stuck your nose in

IRINA: Well someone had to take charge

ANDREI: I was in charge

IRINA: Well I didn't want an incident like last time

ANDREI: What's that supposed to mean?

YURI: She means the shares from the government, the ones you sold to the Russians

ANDREI: I only did what everyone else was doing

IRINA: If you hadn't been in such a rush to sell them on, we might have made some money

ANDREI: How was I to know they'd be worth anything?

IRINA: Well those Russians seemed to know alright. Especially that young fella what was always on about the football, what was his name?

YURI: Abramovich

VLADIMIR enters.

IRINA: I want you all to get along. I can't be doing with all these strains and stresses, be nice to Vladi

YURI: Vladi, she says!

VLADIMIR: Boys, I know this has been an eventful few months, and perhaps we got off on the wrong foot, but I want you to know my intentions towards your mother are entirely honourable

ANDREI: You just want to get your end away

VLADIMIR: I think of you as my sons. I want you to think of me as your father, please – call me daddy

YURI: I'm not calling you daddy

VLADIMIR: You're right, it's confusing enough when your mother calls me that

YURI: *(To ANDREI.)* You're on your own

ANDREI: Yuri, Yuri, don't do anything rash

YURI storms off.

IRINA: I'll see he's alright

IRINA goes after YURI.

ANDREI: Where is this contact of yours?

VLADIMIR: My dear boy, you can't rush these things

ANDREI: Yuri's picked up some transmissions on his receiver. The Americans and the Russians are nearby

VLADIMIR: Are you sure?

ANDREI: Does the phrase 'That's so good I'll play it again' followed by a squall of noise mean anything to you?

VLADIMIR: Sounds like a code. Look, I'll get on to my contact, it's just so hard to get through. That bloody queue in the post office

ANDREI: Who is your contact?

VLADIMIR: The Chechens

ANDREI: I know where they're from, who are they?

VLADIMIR: I can't tell you that

ANDREI: I need something to go on

VLADIMIR: He's called Dennis

ANDREI: Dennis? What kind of name is that for a Chechen?

VLADIMIR: I don't know, I haven't met him

ANDREI: What do you mean you haven't met him? I thought he was your contact?

VLADIMIR: No, he's the contact of my contact

ANDREI: What?

VLADIMIR: I have a contact for the contact

ANDREI: Don't try me, Vladimir

VLADIMIR: My first contact's going to put me in touch with the second contact – the Chechen who'll buy the missile

ANDREI: Dennis the Chechen

VLADIMIR: Yes

ANDREI: So who's your contact? Please tell me you know more about him

VLADIMIR: Of course I do

ANDREI: So what's his name?

VLADIMIR: Ivan

Pause.

ANDREI: Ivan who?

VLADIMIR: He doesn't have a second name

ANDREI: There's quite a lot of Ivans round here, Vladimir, it's the Ukraine

VLADIMIR: He has a nickname

ANDREI: What's his nickname?

VLADIMIR: Russian Ivan. Though I think he's actually Ukrainian. He has a twitch.

ANDREI: What kind of twitch?

VLADIMIR: A distinctive twitch

ANDREI: Show me

VLADIMIR demonstrates the twitch.

That is distinctive

VLADIMIR: That's all I can give you

ANDREI: We have to move fast. Yuri's got some idea in his head about finding his own contact

VLADIMIR: It's not possible, you don't tell these people when it happens, they tell you

ANDREI: Two days, Vladimir, that's all you're getting. Else you'll be disappearing, contacts or no contacts

VLADIMIR: Alright, alright

ANDREI: What if I gave you a better deal?

VLADIMIR: What do you mean?

ANDREI: What deal are you getting with mother?

VLADIMIR: An even split

ANDREI: An even split!

VLADIMIR: We share everything

ANDREI: What if I were to beat that and you deal with me instead?

VLADIMIR: I couldn't possibly betray her

ANDREI: Sixty-forty in your favour

VLADIMIR: Done

4

VLADIMIR and ANDREI stand with DENNIS and two heavies. The heavies hold two briefcases each.

ANDREI: So you're the contact?

DENNIS: Yes

ANDREI: You're Dennis?

DENNIS: That is correct

ANDREI: What kind of name is Dennis for a Chechen?

DENNIS: It's a nickname

VLADIMIR: Just you?

DENNIS: The rest of my men are waiting with the truck, as we agreed

VLADIMIR: First tell me who your contact is

DENNIS: Why?

VLADIMIR: So I can be sure you are who you say you are

DENNIS: How do I know you're who you say you are?

VLADIMIR: You first

DENNIS: No you first

VLADIMIR: No you first

DENNIS: Ivan

VLADIMIR: Ivan who?

DENNIS: Russian Ivan

VLADIMIR: Ivan with the twitch?

Both DENNIS and VLADIMIR perform the distinctive twitch.

DENNIS: Ah! So you are Vladimir
This is the missile?

ANDREI: No, that's the spare missile, the one we're selling is back near the house

DENNIS: You have another missile?

ANDREI: Of course not! How many missiles do you think I have

DENNIS: Ah! You are making a joke. You are very funny, like Said Dudaev

ANDREI: Who's Said Dudaev?

DENNIS: He was my favourite comedian, you know him?

ANDREI: No

DENNIS: That's because he's dead. You know how he died?

ANDREI: No

DENNIS: I killed him. You know why I killed him?

ANDREI: No

DENNIS: Neither do I. You have any more jokes?

ANDREI: No

DENNIS: Good, we don't have time to hang around. We hear the Americans and the Russians are looking for this

VLADIMIR: Is that the money?

DENNIS: No, we just carry cases for fun. See, now I am comedian

ANDREI: Why do you want the missile?

VLADIMIR: Why do you think they want it, it's a bloody missile!

DENNIS: Uranium. What do you think, we can't fire this thing, it's been out here for god knows how long, you have any idea the failure rates? You'd be lucky to get ten percent of these off the ground

ANDREI: What do you want uranium for?

DENNIS: War is dirty. The less you know the better for you it is. Do you want the money or not?

VLADIMIR: Yes

DENNIS barks something in Arabic at his heavies. They speak into walkie-talkies.

ANDREI: Who are they talking to?

DENNIS: I can't carry this on my own

ANDREI: What's to stop them killing us and making off with the thing?

DENNIS: Nothing

Pause.

Although it would be most unethical

ANDREI: You're buying a nuclear missile for uranium

DENNIS: As a rule, in my line of work it doesn't do to have a reputation for a bad deal

IRINA appears.

Who is this?

ANDREI: What are you doing here, I told you to stay inside?

IRINA: I can't find your brother anywhere

ANDREI: Well that's probably for the best, mother will you go inside, it's not safe

DENNIS: This is your mother?

ANDREI: Mum, we're totally doing an international arms deal here, this is really embarrassing

IRINA: You must be Dennis

DENNIS: Madam, you look like their sister

IRINA: Is there a Mrs Dennis?

DENNIS: Only my mother

ANDREI: Mum!

VLADIMIR: I am here, you know

*DENNIS barks an order in Arabic. The heavies hand over the cases
to VLADIMIR. Both IRINA and ANDREI step forward.*

DENNIS: We split it just how you asked

IRINA: Not so fast, I'll take that

ANDREI: I think you'll find that's mine

IRINA: We had a deal. Tell him Vladimir.
Vladimir?

ANDREI: He told me you offered fifty per cent. I gave him a
better deal

IRINA: Fifty? I offered him forty because you'd offered him
thirty

ANDREI: Thirty? We offered him twenty in the first place

VLADIMIR: Sixty-forty. Sorry, Irina, all's fair in love and war.
Andrei, a pleasure doing business with you

ANDREI: Don't worry, mother, you'll get your share, but I'm in
charge of dividing it up. It's not that I don't trust you, but –
well, I don't trust you

*YURI appears on top of the missile, pointing a gun at VLADIMIR.
The heavies aim weapons at YURI.*

YURI: Not so fast! I think we can do a little better

DENNIS: Who the hell is this?

ANDREI: This is my idiot brother. Yuri, get down from there,
you'll get us all killed

YURI: You, what's your name?

DENNIS: Dennis

YURI: Dennis?

ANDREI: He's Chechen

VLADIMIR: It's a nickname

YURI: Here's what's going to happen. Dennis, you're going to deal with me instead of with Vladimir. In return you get to keep one of those cases of money

ANDREI: Why are you giving him money back?

YURI: We don't need the Russian

DENNIS: Yuri – may I call you Yuri? You may have noticed I am an international arms dealer. The clue to this is that I am buying a nuclear missile from you. I do not take orders from people. They take orders from me. On the other hand, I haven't seen testicles as big as yours since I tortured a rapist in Chernokozovo

YURI: You did time in Chernokozovo?

DENNIS: Four years. So I will take you up on your offer

ANDREI: I thought as a rule you didn't double-cross people

DENNIS: Hm, more of a guideline

ANDREI produces a gun which he points at YURI.

ANDREI: Yuri, I won't let you ruin this

VLADIMIR produces his gun which he points at YURI.

VLADIMIR: That's right, Yuri, put the gun down

IRINA produces her gun which she points at ANDREI.

IRINA: Don't you dare point a gun at your brother

ANDREI: Mother, where did you get that?

IRINA: In the cupboard next to the fishing rods

YURI: Andrei, mother, trust me. I'll give you a share of my money

ANDREI: You've already negotiated less money, where's the sense in going with you?

YURI: It's not less if it's split three ways

VLADIMIR: But there's four of us

YURI: That can change Vladimir

ANDREI thinks about this then shifts his gun to VLADIMIR.

VLADIMIR: How could you?

DENNIS: If we leave them long enough, maybe they keep driving the price down

VLADIMIR: Irina. We can be together

IRINA: All's fair in love and war

IRINA follows suit and shifts her gun to VLADIMIR. Now VLADIMIR is pointing his gun at YURI. IRINA, ANDREI and YURI are pointing theirs at VLADIMIR.

DENNIS: You guys talk among yourselves. I'm happy to buy from whoever thinks they're in charge

VLADIMIR puts his gun down.

IRINA: Looks like you're dealing with us now

DENNIS: Done

Suddenly, bursts of gunfire. Explosions. Flashes of light. Smoke. A helicopter. Russian and American soldiers storm the stage, ordering ANDREI, YURI, IRINA, VLADIMIR and DENNIS to kneel at gunpoint. The effect is dizzying. Amid the chaos, an officer checks markings on the missile with notes on a clipboard. The helicopter moves away. Troops lead the Chechens off at gunpoint and train their weapons on YURI, ANDREI, IRINA and VLADIMIR.

Silence.

JOHNSON: Good day to you, I am Captain Johnson Gains, US Army, and today it is my privilege to greet you on behalf of this joint US-Russian operation to reclaim missile SS20 Z seven niner six four two which...

The officer with the clipboard nods at JOHNSON.

...this is

IRINA: What in Trotsky's name is this?

ANDREI: The Americans

YURI: And the Russians

VLADIMIR: My unit

JOHNSON: And Doctor Mihailovich, what a pleasure to see you again

VLADIMIR: That's Major Doctor Mihailovich to you

JOHNSON: Not any more. Boys and girls, will you escort the doctor for debriefing

A couple of troops march VLADIMIR off.

VLADIMIR: Please, you're making a mistake! This is all a terrible mistake!

JOHNSON: He'll be fine – conventions et cetera. We thought we'd never find this thing. Luckily for us, we were able to track a radio signal and here we are, oh my the look on your faces

IRINA: Radio signal?

ANDREI: The receiver, Yuri, you idiot

JOHNSON: Rest assured your cooperation will not pass without due recognition.

JOHNSON presents YURI with a document. YURI, ANDREI and IRINA still have guns pointed at them.

Now if you wouldn't mind signing here... Thank you so much

JOHNSON asks YURI to sign in triplicate. He complies. JOHNSON hands them a small packet.

And also... Thank you so much...and the third one is for you to keep. Receipt's in the envelope. Oh, and – this didn't happen.

JOHNSON exits. The sound of engines roaring into life, a truck reversing. The SS20 and conflat are removed. We hear a helicopter. Orders are shouted and the troops leave the stage as suddenly as they arrived.

All is quiet. ANDREI takes the envelope from YURI. He opens it. A single bill.

ANDREI: A one hundred dollar bill

YURI: And a note

IRINA: What does it say?

ANDREI: Thank you for your cooperation – in two languages

THERE WAS A MAN, THERE WAS NO MAN.

by Colin Teevan

First production

The Tricycle Theatre, London, 16th February 2012

Characters / Cast

AMIRA (Meir's sister, 40)	Shereen Martin
MEIR (Amira's brother, 35)	Daniel Rabin
GULLY (Mahmoud's sister, 35)	Nathalie Armin
MAHMOUD (Gully's brother, 50)	Paul Bhattacharjee

Two men from Sepah, the Iranian secret police.

Director   *Nicolas Kent*

For Helen, David, Roger and Joyce.

PROLOGUE

Dark.

The sound of cars revving, horns beeping and people shouting in Farsi. A motorbike weaving in and out of the traffic is foregrounded. It screeches to a stop. Then speeds off.

Beat.

An explosion followed by screaming, shouting. A woman's voice, GULLY's, is heard howling, crying for help, above the hubbub.

Lights rise and sound fades to:

ZURICH

Silence.

A hotel bedroom: bed, armchair, dressing table, upright chair.

A woman, AMIRA, 40, Middle-Eastern origin, elegantly dressed, professional, with warm overcoat over her arm, sits on the bed, handbag on her lap. Having reached an impasse in the argument she has been having, she looks resolutely front.

MEIR, 35, short and bullish, intelligent, stands. Nothing like AMIRA, yet there is a similarity.

The similarity is there too when they speak, a similarity of vowel and emphasis, but also a difference. While both accents are unplacable, his tends towards the Levant, while hers towards Central Europe.

They have been arguing. They have now reached the crux of the matter, hence the silence.

At length:

AMIRA: You *wanted* me to steal it.

MEIR holds his counsel and regards her steadily.

AMIRA: In Tel Aviv, at Papa's funeral in September, when I told you I'd be seeing the Professor, 'my' Professor at the conference in Jordan, you were so keen to show me the USB, to let me know that 'my' Professor and his friends in the Iranian opposition would be very interested in what it contained.

MEIR: So it's my fault you took it?

AMIRA: You practically begged me to take it. I figured maybe you wanted to help the opposition.

MEIR shrugs.

AMIRA: Don't get me wrong. I do not mean to imply that I thought you capable of an ethical position, but I figured maybe, for once, our interests coincided. But then Ahmadinejad said Monday night, when he announced the assassination, that Israel had breached the computer system that controls their enrichment facility. I know their system's not on the net. It would have had to have been through something like a USB.

MEIR smiles.

MEIR: I'd heard something of that virus. It's a nice piece of work. But I'm afraid we can't take credit for it.

AMIRA: Why? Because if you did you'd have twenty other governments come after you? Because initially you'd sent your little virus round the world on the internet, hoping it would find a way in. But all you succeeded in doing was infecting every Siemens centrifuge system in the world apart from the Iranians, because their system is not on the net. So you had to revert to plan B. Find someone who had access to the system to introduce the virus. The Professor, he was plan B. And I was the mule.

MEIR: You've no proof the USB you stole from me caused this.

AMIRA: I should have known it was a trick. With you and your Mossad friends there's always a trick. A trick behind the trick. He wasn't a loyalist like Ahmadinejad said. He was with the opposition. He was a good guy. You wouldn't understand. It's ethical.

MEIR: Ethics are all very well from the safety of Switzerland, Sis, with your Swiss Alps to protect you. This is an existential issue. It's too important for ethics.

AMIRA: It was an existential issue for him too. You killed him.

MEIR: *(Shrugs.) Yeki bood, yeki-nabood.* There was a man, there was no man.

AMIRA: I know what it means, Meir, I was brought up on Persian fairy tales too.

MEIR: Then you'll know how it continues, Amira.

AMIRA: *Gheir az Khoda, heech-kee nabood.*

MEIR: Other than God there is no one.

AMIRA: You're saying his murder was an act of God?

MEIR: I'm saying *I* killed no man.

AMIRA: You, Mossad. Ahmadinejad said on TV. The Professor's wife appeared too. She was right by him when he died. She told how Israeli agents approached the car on a motorbike as they were stuck in traffic, stuck a bomb to the door. His blood was still spattered on her face and scarf –

MEIR: Your Professor's wife *also* described him as a loyal servant of the Islamic Republic of Iran –

AMIRA: What lies someone tells after his death doesn't change the fact that you killed an innocent man. No doubt they made her say that.

MEIR: If anyone killed him, Amira, you did with your good intentions.

AMIRA: What's that supposed to mean?

MEIR does not respond.

AMIRA: Meir?

MEIR: What did you talk about at the conference in Amman?

AMIRA: What do you mean *I* killed him?

Beat. MEIR turns to face AMIRA full on.

MEIR: Do you think I travelled two thousand miles, do you think my superiors let me travel two thousand miles, because your liberal conscience is in a twist?

Beat.

AMIRA: No, I think you travelled two thousand miles to stop me going public about your virus.

MEIR: You stole some top secret information. Some of my colleagues think you're a traitor.

AMIRA: I did what you wanted.

MEIR: The outcome might be to our advantage, but your intentions were treacherous.

AMIRA: So not only do you want me to do your bidding, but you want me to do it willingly?

MEIR: You are still an Israeli citizen and you have had contact with an enemy scientist. A scientist our enemies publicly admit was working on their illegal nuclear programme.

AMIRA: But you know and I know he wasn't –

MEIR: *(Shrugs.)* I'm happy to take them at face value on this one.

AMIRA: We know he was working on energy cycles.

MEIR: *(Checks watch.)* What did you talk about at the conference, Amira? I need to know what he told you.

Pause.

AMIRA: And if I choose not to tell you? If I choose to go public? What will you do? Kidnap me? Take me back to Israel? Throw me in prison? *(Beat.)* What if I lie?

MEIR: I'll know the truth by the lies you tell, sister.

AMIRA: Seems like you don't need me then to know what to think, brother.

Beat.

MEIR: What did you and your Professor talk about? We know you approached him after his paper.

AMIRA wary now, realising she was being watched.

MEIR: Good paper was it?

AMIRA: No. Not really.

MEIR: Alpha particles. *(Beat.)* The alpha particle is the radiation particle itself, isn't it? It's spat out of an unstable nucleus. Two protons and two neutrons. Helium. But ironically, in itself, it is the most stable of particles. Very difficult to split. Out of instability, stability, one might say. Though to achieve stability the nucleus must go through the violence of the 'spitting out'.

Beat.

AMIRA: Who needs scientists when you've got Wikipedia?

MEIR: What was his angle?

Beat.

AMIRA: He claimed he'd discovered a new cycle which would lead to clean safe energy for all. The theory, such as it was, was thrown out in the West in the Sixties.

MEIR: And after his paper you went to your room?

AMIRA: It had been a long day. I was tired.

MEIR: Together.

Beat.

AMIRA: He wanted a drink. He said my room was the only place *his* people weren't watching him.

MEIR: And what did you talk about, over drinks, in your room?

Beat. MEIR checks his watch.

My return flight to Tel Aviv is in an hour, Sister. I want to know what was said in that room. I want to know what they know.

AMIRA: Or else what?

MEIR: I might not be able to stop my colleagues telling your husband about 'your' Professor.

AMIRA: What is there to tell him except that my brother had him killed?

MEIR: We all crave our security, you your Swiss banker, me a non-nuclear Middle-East.

AMIRA snorts.

AMIRA: Don't go all peacenik on me, Meir, you love it. Don't pretend you don't. The bluffing, double-bluffing game of it all. The 'we don't have a bomb but we really do' and 'you don't have one but you're pretending that you do', and 'we know that you're pretending but we'll choose to believe it because that way we can keep playing the game'. Little boys. You'd be lost without your games.

Pause.

AMIRA: You want to know what we did in my room? We played chess.

MEIR looks at her. She holds his gaze.

MEIR: Saw yourselves as some kind of Spassky and Fischer?

AMIRA does not rise to it.

MEIR: OK. What did you talk about while you played chess?

Beat.

AMIRA: Alpha particles.

MEIR: I told you, I'll know the truth by the lies you tell.

AMIRA: OK, I'll admit it, we talked about quantum tunnelling too.

MEIR is blank.

AMIRA: What's wrong. Not do all your homework, little brother?

MEIR: Enlighten me.

AMIRA: How a particle, inextricably bound to a nucleus, no matter how high it jumps or hard it pushes, cannot break its bounds, yet might suddenly find itself outside that nucleus. Giving the appearance of being in two places at the one time.

MEIR: And politics? You didn't talk politics?

AMIRA: I'm a scientist, Meir, a Swiss scientist for God's sake.

MEIR: Everything is politics, sister, even no-politics is politics. Sitting in your chalet in the Alps with your Mercedes in the drive and your banker husband and your two blond children and your fridge full of Swiss chocolate, that's politics. And fucking an Iranian nuclear physicist is most definitely politics –

AMIRA: I –

AMIRA stops herself.

AMIRA: I will not even stoop to deny that.

MEIR: Too much security breeds illusions. I don't have any illusions. There isn't the space where *I* live. What we see is the world as it is, not as we'd like it.

AMIRA: Every paranoid schizophrenic is convinced he sees the world as it is.

MEIR: So we're imagining the hundreds of rockets launched each year at us by Hizbollah? And where do these two-bit Shia thugs get them? Your friends in Iran that's where.

AMIRA: He was in the opposition, a Green, a reformer.

MEIR: Hardliner or opposition, they're all the same when it comes to us. They want to see us obliterated.

AMIRA: It's not about you, why can't you understand that? It's about them. What they experienced. Being alone in the world, surrounded by enemies, just like Israel. That's what we talked about.

MEIR: So you did talk politics?

AMIRA: So what if I did? Why can't you look at it from their perspective?

MEIR: Because I'm sane. I cannot take up a perspective that is insane. That would be contradictory.

AMIRA laughs.

AMIRA: 'We will not be the first to use nuclear weapons in the Middle-East, but we will not be the second,' Israeli official policy. And that's not contradictory?

MEIR: That is a paradox, not a contradiction.

AMIRA shakes her head.

MEIR: A paradox may contain a deeper truth beyond the simple logic of language.

AMIRA: How very convenient to base your nuclear policy on a truth beyond logic or language.

MEIR: You physicists live with paradoxes. You claim that light is both a wave and a particle. You say that is a paradox but not a contradiction, because there can be no truth in a contradiction.

AMIRA: *(Relenting.)* He too feared Iran developing the bomb.

MEIR looks at her.

AMIRA: That's what we talked about in my room, in Amman. He said he feared that when Iran developed the bomb, that would be an end to democracy. The Revolutionary Guard and the secret police, the Sepah, they already have the country sewn up, he said, monopolies over most industries, protection rackets on every small business. With the bomb, he said, they will no longer be responsible to the Supreme Leader. The people will live in fear. The Shah wanted nuclear warheads for just the same reason. Absolute power. Against the world, yes, but also against his own people. It will be the Shah's regime by another name, he said. What our own father fought against. That's why I gave him the USB. *(Pause.)* Don't you care what becomes of them? You're Iranian Meir, do you forget? You and I are both Iranian.

MEIR: Just because I was born in a stable does not mean I'm a horse.

AMIRA: Don't you remember? Our father went out on the roof of our building in Teheran in '79 and shouted *Allah-uh akbhar* against the Shah when Khomeini commanded it.

MEIR: And then Khomeini thanked him by closing his business and our school, and restricting our rights to travel.

AMIRA: And Israel rescued us!

MEIR: They offered us a life, security and education.

AMIRA: As long as we became paid up members –

MEIR: And this is how you repay them? By betraying them?

AMIRA: I didn't betray them… I was trying to help.

MEIR can barely conceal his contempt.

AMIRA: And he was…

AMIRA is caught by surprise by her emotions.

AMIRA: He was…

AMIRA breaks off.

MEIR: What? What were you going to say?

AMIRA: Nothing. I was only going to say he *was* a good guy. That's all. That's all there is to it. And you set me up, and I set him up. You disgust me. And make me disgust myself.

AMIRA tries to distract herself from her tears by rummaging in her bag for a tissue. She cannot find any tissues in her handbag.

AMIRA: I need a glass of water.

MEIR looks at her suspiciously, then relents. He goes to the bathroom and fills a glass of water. AMIRA composes herself. MEIR returns from the bathroom and hands her a glass of water. She drinks, more thirsty than she thought she was.

AMIRA: Why did you have to kill him? He was an asset surely.

Beat.

MEIR: Some things cannot be helped.

AMIRA: You're going?

AMIRA: Aren't you going to torture me at least? Pull out my fingernails? Put my head under water?

MEIR: Why? I know the truth.

AMIRA: What is that?

MEIR: You loved him.

Beat. AMIRA is thrown.

AMIRA: So? What's to stop me talking all the same? What's to stop me telling the world about the virus? Getting all those governments whose systems you've infected on your case? You'll become a pariah nation.

MEIR: *(Shrugs.)* So what's new?

AMIRA: What's to stop me?

MEIR: Because we will out you as an Iranian spy. Those who view us as a pariah will continue to view us as such and those that don't will believe us. And as for you, your husband the banker will learn of your affair. Like I said, Sis, we all need our security.

AMIRA: *(Wearily.)* What affair?

MEIR looks at her.

MEIR: My guess is he reminded you of Papa. The smell of cardamon and black tea. See, I do remember. And a good guy. By that I mean naive. A fantasist.

AMIRA slaps him. He does not flinch.

MEIR: It must be tough, Sis, not being able to share your heartbreak with anyone. Except me. And I'm hardly a sympathetic listener.

MEIR checks watch.

I've got a plane to catch.

AMIRA: Why did you do it, Meir?

MEIR bites his tongue.

AMIRA: So all Iranians know you mean business? That you can get two men into downtown Teheran in rush hour? Take out a leading scientist in broad daylight?

Beat.

MEIR: Something like that.

MEIR turns to go.

AMIRA: He was just a pawn. He opened up their whole system to you and then you sacrificed him. Just another piece in a game. But a man, not a piece, has died here. We can't just start a new game when everyone's been blown from the board.

MEIR: You and I aren't that different. We are still the two kids looking for a home. We just look for it in different ways. Love to Hans and Heidi.

MEIR goes to the door.

AMIRA: David and Hannah. Your nephew and niece are called –

She looks about but MEIR has gone.

AMIRA: David and Hannah.

AMIRA sits on the bed. She wipes a tear from her eye, braces herself, takes out a pocket mirror and adjusts hair and lipstick to brave the world again. She takes one last look around the room and leaves.

Beat.

TEHERAN

Two men in cheap, dark suits, white shirts, no ties, enter, dragging a woman, GULLY, 35, dressed in an elegant Teheran-style hijab. GULLY is in a state of shock. Some might recognise the men as Sepah, Iranian secret police. They sit her on the bed. The two men proceed to check the room for bugs.

GULLY looks up, terrified. Her face and hijab are spattered in blood.

MAHMOUD, 50, bearded, less cheap dark suit, but still white shirt, no tie, appears in doorway and watches the men.

MAHMOUD enters.

The two Sepah men have finished checking the place.

MAHMOUD: Clean?

They nod.

MAHMOUD: Leave us.

They leave the room and wait outside the door. MAHMOUD closes the door.

Silence.

MAHMOUD: Has your hearing returned?

Silence. GULLY looks up trying to figure out where she is, and whether she is being addressed.

MAHMOUD: Can you hear me, sister?

GULLY looks at him. Is it deafness or fear? When he catches her eye, she looks away. MAHMOUD checks watch.

GULLY: Was it them?

MAHMOUD: Good. You can hear.

GULLY: Was it Israel?

MAHMOUD: We don't have much time.

GULLY: But why would the Israelis kill my husband?

MAHMOUD: It depends.

GULLY: On what?

MAHMOUD: On you.

GULLY looks at him.

GULLY: I need a glass of water, my throat is dry.

MAHMOUD regards GULLY. MAHMOUD goes to the bathroom. We hear him fill a glass of water.

MAHMOUD: *(Off.)* We really don't have much time.

MAHMOUD returns, passes GULLY the glass. GULLY drinks greedily.

MAHMOUD: Feeling better?

GULLY: Why does who killed him depend on me?

MAHMOUD: *(Ignoring her.)* I need to know what you know.

GULLY looks at him.

GULLY: *(Steeling herself, defiant.)* All I know is that we were in our car, driving to the Institute, and two men on a motorbike pulled up beside us at the lights at Revolution Square. They stuck something on his car door, something magnetic and drove off. And he had just enough time to understand what it was, and to turn to me and say sorry… Or at least I think that's what I think I know. Are you going to tell me something else happened? Is that why you and your Sepah friends have brought me here, to this hotel? *(Beat.)* I should be with him, Mahmoud, I want to be with my husband.

MAHMOUD: *(Checks watch.)* His body will be at the hospital by now. I'll take you to him after.

GULLY: After what?

MAHMOUD: After! After!

GULLY: You *are* one of them, aren't you? Sepah, the secret police? We always suspected. Tell me, why did Israel kill him? He was working on a clean energy cycle. He was not designing bombs. He was not political. Whose side are you on, Mahmoud?

MAHMOUD: I have taken a great risk in bringing you here. I need to know about the conference in Amman.

GULLY: He told me nothing.

MAHMOUD: I'm trying to help you.

GULLY: And how do you propose helping me? Pull out my finger nails until I admit my husband was a spy? But if he was, why would they kill him?

GULLY stands up.

GULLY: You cannot help me.

GULLY goes to leave. MAHMOUD grabs her by the arm and pushes her down.

MAHMOUD: Your husband attended the Sesame conference in Amman in September as a representative of the Islamic Republic. He gave a paper on alpha particles. Afterwards he was approached by the physicist Dr. Amira Bergman-Tinner of the Nieman Institute, Zurich. Naturalised Swiss, but born in the Jewish quarter of Teheran. We have a photo of them together.

MAHMOUD puts a photo on the table.

MAHMOUD: She then invited him back to her room.

GULLY looks at MAHMOUD. He holds her gaze. She shakes her head slowly.

GULLY: I know you never liked him, Mahmoud, but he was a good man.

MAHMOUD takes out a cassette tape, he places it on the table. AMIRA looks at him.

MAHMOUD: A recording we made.

MAHMOUD looks to GULLY for a reaction.

MAHMOUD: He had sexual relations with this woman.

GULLY: No –

GULLY looks at MAHMOUD steadily attempting to maintain her dignity.

GULLY: Why should I believe you? You have lied about who you are and what you do all your life.

MAHMOUD: And what about you? What about him?

MAHMOUD takes out a portable cassette-recorder. He loads the cassette, presses play and passes GULLY the headphones.

GULLY knocks the headphones from his hand.

GULLY: I have just watched my husband die in front of me. His blood is on my clothes, my face – You are my brother, Mahmoud, why?

MAHMOUD forces one speaker of the headphone violently over her ear. GULLY listens defiantly.

GULLY: It's not him.

MAHMOUD: It is.

GULLY: I was married to him for fifteen years, I can tell.

MAHMOUD shakes his head. He puts the cassette-recorder on the table.

GULLY: Why are you doing this? What do you want from me? To tell you he was a traitor? You want me to believe he was something he was not? He believed in the Islamic Republic. He offered up his whole life for the Islamic Republic. In '79 he was one of the first students to defy the Shah to take to the streets to support Khomeini. And when Iraq attacked us, he gave up his place studying literature and enlisted in the army. He fought for eight years in that war. Then, when it was over and he returned to the University, although he loved poetry, the Islamic Republic needed scientists, so he studied physics to help the Republic.

MAHMOUD: He's with the opposition, little Sister.

GULLY: The opposition still believe in the Islamic Republic. It is not a crime to support the opposition in a republic.

MAHMOUD: We are surrounded by enemies. They will exploit any sign of dissent. In Amman the woman Bergman-Tinner gave him something.

GULLY: No.

MAHMOUD: A USB. After Amman, did he ever show you a USB?

GULLY does not answer.

MAHMOUD: Did he give you a USB to look after?

GULLY does not answer.

GULLY: What is so important about this USB? He's dead.

MAHMOUD: We believe the USB contained information for the opposition about the Secret Police. Lies. The kind of lies the opposition like to spread about us. That is why we watched him. But that is not serious. We would have squashed those lies like ants. But that is not why our enemies gave it to him. They gave it to him because they wanted him to look at this information on his computer at the Institute. Because his computer is inside the nuclear programme's system, and the USB contained a virus that once inside the system ran from one machine to another, looking for the programmes that operate the centrifuges at the enrichment facilities. Some damage is irreparable.

GULLY: So, this foreign woman tricked him.

MAHMOUD: He was guilty of sabotage, of treason.

GULLY: He was guilty of being tricked.

MAHMOUD: We checked *your* computer at home. We found traces of the virus on it too.

Beat. GULLY absorbs the implication.

GULLY: You were in my home?

MAHMOUD continues to look at her.

GULLY: *(Weakening.)* Maybe he…maybe *he* used it –

MAHMOUD goes over to the recorder and unplugs the headphones. He turns it on full blast so we hear the muffled, buzzy alleged recording of AMIRA and the Professor making love in Amman. GULLY attempts to maintain her dignity. She covers her ears. MAHMOUD sits down beside her and pulls her hands away from her ears. He hisses in her ear so as not to be heard by colleagues outside the door or recording devices.

MAHMOUD: I took a great risk bringing you here. *(Beat.)* My superiors don't know about your computer.

GULLY attempts not to betray her fear.

MAHMOUD: They still wanted a bomb big enough to kill both of you.

GULLY looks at him. Long pause.

MAHMOUD: But I persuaded them that you could be persuaded.

Pause.

GULLY: Persuaded to do what?

MAHMOUD turns off the cassette-recorder.

MAHMOUD: When we first came in, you asked if Israel had killed him. Why?

GULLY: *(Fearful.)* Because…because he is an Iranian nuclear scientist.

MAHMOUD nods.

MAHMOUD: So, like I said, it depends on you. We agree it's Israel, then the President will go on television tonight with you, he will describe your husband as a great scientist and patriot, and denounce his murder as the work of Israeli assassins. You and your children will able to continue to live in the comfort and security you presently enjoy. Though of course you will relinquish your post at the Institute, and you will keep me informed as to your contact with friends and colleagues in the opposition.

GULLY: And if not? If I don't go along with your story?

MAHMOUD: You will die en route to the hospital of your injuries. Your children, they will be sent to a state orphanage.

GULLY looks at him in terror.

GULLY: They are your nephew and niece.

MAHMOUD stands.

MAHMOUD: Do you think I'm doing this for you?

MAHMOUD produces a USB.

MAHMOUD: We found this in your bag in the car.

GULLY has no choice but she will not give MAHMOUD the satisfaction of seeing her break.

GULLY: But surely the Israelis, will deny it.

MAHMOUD: *(Shakes his head.)* We know our enemy. We know how they think. Because they think like us. And we are sure they'll think it in their interests to let the world believe it was them?

Pause.

GULLY: You conspire with your enemy to keep your own people in fear?

MAHMOUD does not answer.

GULLY: You fear internal opposition more than you fear your enemies?

MAHMOUD turns off the cassette. GULLY stands up with as much dignity as she can muster.

GULLY: He used to explain the nucleus of the uranium atom to his students. He asked them to imagine 92 cars and 143 trailers chained together, all revving and revving and pulling in different directions but none able to break free. Like the traffic in Revolution Square at rush hour. But then you fire another trailer into it and one chain rips, and because of this one little tear, the whole thing roars and rips and splits in a cloud of dust and petrol fumes and noise. This is like the society you have created, brother. Be careful it does not blow up on you.

He goes the door. The two Sepah men wait outside.

MAHMOUD: These two men will take you to the hospital. To the back entrance. It will appear as if you were with your husband all this time.

MAHMOUD leaves. The two Sepah men step inside to take her.

But GULLY doesn't listen. As AMIRA had done when we first saw her. She sits on the bed looking resolutely front.

AXIS
by Diana Son

First production
The Tricycle Theatre, London, 16th February 2012

Characters / Cast

MAN	Tariq Jordan
WOMAN	Nathalie Armin
PARK	Simon Chandler
LEE	David Yip

Director   *Tara Robinson*

Setting
Scene 1 – the White House, during George Bush's administration.
Scene 2 – the Executive Office of Kim Jong-un.

SCENE 1

A cramped office in the White House, in December 2001. Two men are watching a replay of George W. Bush giving a speech on their crappy TV.

BUSH: *(On TV.)* 'And on behalf of the American people, I thank the many world leaders who have called to offer their condolences and assistance. America and our friends and allies join with all those who want peace and security in the world, and we stand together to win the war against terrorism.'

The MAN turns off the TV and faces his boss.

MAN: 'The war against terrorism.' 'The war against terrorism.' You know what I hate about that phrase?

WOMAN: That you didn't write it.

MAN: How do we wage a war against terrorism. Terrorism is a tactic, not an entity. It's like saying we're going to wage a war against sneak attacks. There's no enemy. No face to put on a bullseye.

WOMAN: It's catchy, though. And has caught on like wildfire. You can't read an article in the *Washington Post* or *New York Times* that doesn't use it. Especially now that we're in Afghanistan.

MAN: Going after the Taliban was a no-brainer. But if the president wants to convince the American public that we need to push Saddam Hussein out of power, we can't use sloppy phrases like 'the war against terrorism'.

WOMAN: So what've you come up with?

MAN: Just a little something I jotted down in my spare time…

The MAN hands his boss his version of Bush's State of the Union Address, 2002. The WOMAN quickly scans it, reading quietly but out loud to herself.

WOMAN: *(Quickly scanning.)* Afghanistan…confirmed our worst fears…depth of their hatred…madness…troops…weapons of mass destruction…

Beat. Then, his eyes light on a phrase. He looks up.

WOMAN: Axis of hatred?

The MAN nods. He's proud of it. His boss mulls it over – its meaning, musicality, mouthfeel.

WOMAN: Axis of hatred.

The MAN points to a section of the speech.

MAN: And the notion that we can't wait for Saddam, and other rogue and reckless regimes to strike us first. We suspect or know they have nuclear weapons. We have to attack first to protect ourselves and the world. The threat is imminent. I go on to list some of Saddam's atrocities…

The WOMAN looks at the speech.

WOMAN: So this axis of yours, you name Iraq and Iran… the National Security people will like the focus on Iran. Condoleeza says the Iranian people are moving towards revolution. A sign of support from us could embolden them.

MAN: Sure would make things easier for us.

WOMAN: But I hear 'axis' and I think of World War II and that axis alliance, which was three countries, Germany, Italy, and Japan… You only list two.

MAN: There's always Libya. Gaddafi's another nutcase who we think has nukes…made out of gold, probably. Or how about Syria –

WOMAN: Not another Muslim country.

MAN: But we're focussing on states that sponsor terrorism –

WOMAN: We don't want the president to sound anti-Muslim.

MAN: God forbid we offend the people who are attacking us.

WOMAN: You know who you're working for, don't you? President Bush has gone out of his way to show he's not anti-Muslim, he's anti-terrorist. He doesn't want to stir up any negativity towards Muslim Americans.

MAN: The man's got an incredible moral conscience. Believe me, I respect that.

WOMAN: Not to mention, he campaigned hard for the Muslim American vote and they came out for him in a big way.

MAN: I didn't know that.

WOMAN: Fifty thousand Muslims came to the polls in Florida and voted 88 percent for the president. Who knows? Could be Muslim Americans had a big role in him winning.

MAN: God love 'em for it. But something tells me it had less to do with their love of George W. Bush and more to do with the fact that Al Gore had a Jew on his ticket.

WOMAN: *(Already onto another thought.)* Mm.

Beat. He writes on the speech.

WOMAN: North Korea.

MAN: North Korea? What. As part of the axis?

WOMAN: Why not? They're a rogue regime.

MAN: OK, but –

WOMAN: I mean, you don't get any more rogue than that Kim Jong-il. Freaking lunatic.

MAN: But if we say all three countries belong to the same axis, and then present our argument for attacking Iraq.

WOMAN: You worried North Korea will think they're next?

MAN: Technically, we are still at war with them.

WOMAN: Kim has bullied every administration leading up to ours. It's time someone called his bluff.

MAN: But we just got him to agree to put a moratorium on ballistic missile tests.

WOMAN: Well, we know how good his word is.

The WOMAN stands up.

WOMAN: I'll run it by State and the National Security guys, but I think it'll fly.

MAN: *(Trying it out.)* Iraq, Iran and North Korea.
(Quoting his own speech.) 'States like these, and their terrorist allies, constitute an axis of hatred, arming to threaten the peace of the world.' I don't know…there's something not quite –

WOMAN: You're right, you're right. Something's off –

MAN: Bringing Asia into it dilutes the focus. We should stick to the terrorist strongholds, and the reality is that they are / Muslim –

WOMAN: What's that Bible passage the president kept paraphrasing in the days right after 9/11? It was from the New Testament…it's on the tip of my tongue.

MAN: Don't ask me, I'm strictly an Old Testament kind of /guy –

WOMAN: 'Be not overcome by evil, but overcome evil with good.'
Romans 12:21.

He writes on the speech again.

WOMAN: Axis of evil.

MAN: Axis of evil?

WOMAN: Yeah.

Beat.

He's gonna like that.

SCENE TWO

2012 – the future. Two men, LEE and PARK, both in their 50s, enter a room talking. They are mid-conversation.

LEE: I don't trust the Americans. Why now? Did you ask them why now?

PARK: They said they see a moment of opportunity.

LEE: Of course. They think they see a moment of weakness. A young boy with chubby cheeks, who went to school in Switzerland, likes basketball and Michael Jackson –

PARK: Michael Jordan. The Supreme Leader / likes Michael –

LEE: They think he's been tainted by their world so they can corrupt him with their money –

PARK: But we want their money. Our economy is unsustainable. Our people are eating tree bark and grass.

LEE: They'd be eating beef at every meal if these Americans would let us do business with them. Our economy would soar.

PARK: Come on Lee, what business? What would we sell? We don't have any products because we can't power our factories.

LEE: Ah, but the earth has provided for us, my friend.

PARK: You're not going mystical on me, are you, Lee?

LEE: Rare earth minerals. We have 20 million tons of it and the Americans need it to make their cars and computers, their beloved iPads.

PARK: Except that we don't have the money for mining equipment. The minerals are just sitting there. You know we need money to make money.

LEE: I don't want it from the Americans.

PARK: But no one else will come close to the amount we need.

LEE: No. The Americans are bullies. Painting us as a nuclear threat when it's they who have refused to negotiate. And now in our time of mourning, they come knocking on our door with a fist full of cash, ready to buy us out.

PARK: In his last year of life, the Dear Leader told us that for the right price –

LEE: That's funny. I don't remember you being in the room with the Dear Leader during that conversation.

PARK: Maybe I wasn't but he did put me on the negotiating committee. And I was told that if the Americans offered a suitable payment, the Dear Leader would consider it.

LEE: You're forgetting something, aren't you? Wasn't there more to the picture?

PARK: Don't patronise me, Lee. I'm well aware of the conditions, I presented them. American troops out of South Korea, light water reactors for producing fuel and obviously, a peace treaty.

LEE: Obviously. You let the dollar signs cloud your eyes and you lose sight of what's at stake in this, our protection against attack and our self-sufficiency.

PARK: You're wrong. I am well aware it would be suicide to reduce our nuclear capabilities without ending the war.

LEE: Good. Then you'll agree we can't accept the money. In which case it might be better if, when we talk to / Supreme we don't –

PARK: But we *don't* reduce them, we simply put the fuel rods to bed. Our Dear Leader would have accepted the money, allowed the inspectors back in but never disarmed completely. We do the same.

LEE: Our Dear Leader always had our best interests in mind / but we don't know whether Supreme –

PARK: But the Americans have offered us 1.5 billion dollars this time. That's more than 3 times the amount they've offered before. And substantially more than the Chinese give us. I want to advise our Supreme Leader to accept.

LEE: And alienate our Chinese comrades by taking American payoffs?

PARK: Comrades! The Chinese only give us enough aid to keep us from collapsing. They only want us as a buffer state between them and the American military.

LEE: He'll be here soon and we're not on the same page. Can't you see that taking this American money makes us as bad as the South Koreans?

PARK: Lee. 1.5 billion dollars can revive this country. We can manufacture, mine and farm. We can feed the people in the provinces, improve our international / image –

LEE: 1.5 billion doesn't buy 70 years of self-reliance. The people in the provinces, they believe in this country. Hungry as they are, they're proud to be North Koreans and not American puppets.

PARK: Come on Lee, I don't want to be like a South Korean either…

LEE: Our country is the true Korea. Only we can claim a leader who has kept out foreign influence. Our founder and Great Leader was the only Korean in 500 years to keep out the Japanese.

PARK: He was a great leader, I don't disagree with you, he was the true leader, a god on / earth but –

LEE: And then his son, the Dear Leader continued the legacy bringing your mighty and powerful United States to its knees. These Americans you want to trust tried to force us to give up our bombs by cutting off aid, controlling who did business with us, calling us part of their axis of evil and threatening to attack.

PARK: But that was the old president. / The whole world thought he was crazy.

LEE: But this new president has withheld aid, reneged on promises *and* repeated the same cycle as the others – 'give up your bombs or we won't negotiate.' As if we don't understand that if we give them up first, we won't have anything to negotiate with.

PARK: Supreme likes the new president.

LEE: He likes him because he plays basketball. Supreme has tasted too much of the outside world.

Beat.

(Quietly but firmly.) We cannot let him accept this offer.

A knock on the door. An AIDE appears. He is extremely deferential.

AIDE: Excuse me, sirs.

LEE: You're interrupting.

AIDE: Yes, sir. I'm very sorry. But the Supreme Leader is on his way. I thought you should know.

PARK: Where is he coming from?

AIDE: His home. His driver said they'll arrive in less than three minutes. He will pick both of you up in his car and take you to the military academy.

LEE: I knew that. Go. And don't interrupt again.

AIDE: Yes, sir.

The AIDE leaves.

PARK: Perhaps I'm misunderstanding but surely the Supreme Leader will decide for himself whether or not to accept the offer.

LEE: *(Loaded.)* The Supreme Leader will be influenced by the wisdom of his elders. *Most* of us have been guiding this country since before he was born. And we have earned our position. His decision will represent our vision for the country.

PARK: Lee, you may have been in the Dear Leader's inner circle, but Supreme has brought me into his. He has chosen me. And I will serve him as he demands.

Beat. LEE paces uncomfortably.

LEE: But it's not enough.

Pause.

PARK: You've been in this job too long, Lee.

LEE: And you haven't been long enough, Park.

Beat.

PARK: How much more do you want?

LEE: Two billion.

PARK: *(Shaking head.)* Too much. They might take the offer back. It's enough. I know 1.5 billion is an amount the Dear Leader would have considered.

LEE: And the Dear Leader would have taken care of the country *and us* with that amount. *(Glancing towards the door.)* Supreme may not.

PARK: Why not? We're his loyal servants, his uncles, cousins, friends of his father. Why wouldn't he take care of us? He knows how things work.

LEE: He knows how it works with the Chinese, but will the Americans be the same? Won't they watch every cent of their payment?

PARK: I don't know.

LEE: I do.

Beat. LEE hurriedly checks his watch and checks the door.

Do you like your life?

PARK: What on earth do you mean? Lee you're / starting to –

LEE: You like your nice, big house in your walled off compound?

PARK: Well… Yes.

LEE: You like driving your Mercedez Benz.

PARK: Of course I like my car. And so do you.

LEE: Yes and I like the case of Courvoisier I get every New Year. You let Supreme take that money and I may not get it next year.

PARK: Of course you will. It's all part of our tradition. Supreme knows that.

LEE: You trust this boy too much.

PARK: The Dear Leader chose him.

LEE: He was the only one left! The oldest son is an overgrown child, embarrassing us all by sneaking into Disneyland. And the middle son flits around like a little girl. Supreme was his *only* choice and we have no idea if he will uphold his father's tradition.

PARK: He was chosen because he will.

LEE: Maybe. If the Americans *let* him after we've sold our country to them. Do you see?

Beat.

I will not tell Supreme about the offer and neither will you.

PARK: What?

LEE: The offer doesn't exist.

PARK: Is this a set-up?

LEE: We will not allow you to do it.

PARK: Are you trying to frame me? Getting me to…

LEE: I suggest you do what we say. Or you may find you're not needed.

PARK: Who's 'we'?

LEE: You may be Supreme's favourite, Park, but you're not everyone's.

PARK: Are you threatening me?

LEE: Yes.

PARK: I don't believe this, have you lost your mind? I can't withhold an offer from the head of state –

LEE: You can if it's in your country's best interest.

PARK: You mean, in my own personal best interest. And yours –

LEE: They are one and the same.

PARK: This is…this is… Look, I think we should forget what you just said.

LEE: Use your head, Park. Think about what's at risk here. What if he leaves?

PARK: Leaves? The son of Kim Jong-il?

LEE: Yes. What if the spoiled fat rich kid takes off.

PARK: How dare you speak about our leader –

LEE: Decides that 1.5 billion dollars buys him a big mansion in Rangoon and all the protection he needs. He doesn't have to worry about 25 million people, half of whom are dying of hunger.

PARK: They are his children –

LEE: *They're the dirt that gets caught in the grooves of his shoes.* He doesn't care about them, why should he? He's seen the outside world. With 1.5 billion he can go anywhere he likes and live the high life unlike us, we're trapped.

PARK: What do you mean? We're the most privileged people in the state.

LEE: That's exactly my point. We could never have the same kind of lives outside Pyongyang. We'd be nobodies in another country. You want to be a taxi driver in China? A rubbish collector? Go ahead, tell him about the offer. That's where we'll end up.

Beat.

And if that doesn't stop you – think about what would happen to our country if he left. Our beloved homeland would be torn into pieces.

PARK: You need medical help. That's what this is. Some kind of a breakdown –

LEE: The inner circle would erupt into chaos – aunts and uncles stabbing each other in the back, fighting to take the reins. We'd be a nuclear country with no leader.

PARK: It won't happen.

LEE: And China won't pick up the pieces after we've taken American money.

PARK: The Supreme Leader wouldn't abandon his country like that.

LEE: No?

PARK: Lee, are you saying you know something about our Supreme Leader that I don't?

LEE: Do any of us know anything about him?

PARK: *(Hesitates.)* He won't leave, you're being paranoid.

LEE: OK, then, let's say he stays and accepts the money

PARK: Then our country becomes / economically self-sufficient but we –

LEE: *(Overlapping.)* Our country becomes a colony of the United States. Just like the South / and we are left –

PARK: So then, let's say he turns it down, in a show of moral strength.

LEE: As you said yourself, our economy is unsustainable. Our entire situation is unsustainable. Either way, we lose our country. I see that too Park.

Beat.

Think about yourself. I – we – the others and I – *suggest* the offer disappears and we buy ourselves more time.

Pause. PARK stares at LEE.

PARK: But… Lee… I don't – I mean – how could we keep it a secret?

LEE: *(Inhales.)* Well…

The AIDE knocks on the door again.

AIDE: I'm sorry, sir, I know you said not to interrupt, but the Supreme Leader has arrived. He is waiting for you in the car.

The AIDE quickly exits. LEE looks at PARK. PARK looks at LEE. The AIDE comes back in.

(A little bolder.) Sirs, did you hear me? He's *waiting.*

End.

TALK TALK FIGHT FIGHT
by Ryan Craig

First production
The Tricycle Theatre, London, 16th February 2012

Characters / Cast

BARONESS JANET MERCER	Belinda Lang
ANNIE	Shereen Martin
TAZ	Daniel Rabin
CARTER CULLOCH	David Yip
DR. ALI AL-HASHEMI	Paul Bhattacharjee

Director	*Nicolas Kent*

Setting
New York. A pretty soulless conference room at the UN. A table is covered with papers, documents, files, dossiers, books; a couple of laptops, cups of coffee and plates of biscuits.

The room doubles as a hotel room when Hashemi enters, but this should be denoted by a lighting change and little more.

Lights up on ANNIE and TAZ in mid-argument. BARONESS JANET MERCER watches.

TAZ: Power.

ANNIE: OK.

TAZ: Power is why.

ANNIE: Yes.

TAZ: Nuclear Power.

ANNIE: But that doesn't answer my question.

TAZ: Which is?

ANNIE: Which is; if your nuclear programme is purely for civil purposes why enrich twenty times more uranium than you'd need for energy consumption?

TAZ: We're stockpiling. We need to be self-sufficient because of these sanctions of yours.

ANNIE: That doesn't explain why you hide it all under a mountain?

TAZ: To protect our reactors from aerial attack.

ANNIE: But why would they be attacked if they're for peaceful purposes?

TAZ: You don't think destroying our energy supply would harm us?

ANNIE: But your country has the second largest reserves of natural gas and the fourth largest of oil, why would it need nuclear power as well?

TAZ: Because our refineries are still damaged from the war with Iraq.

ANNIE: So fix them.

TAZ: OK fine can we have eighty billion dollars please?

ANNIE: You've already rejected help from the EU on this issue.

TAZ: The EU? The EU is trying to cripple my country with sanctions?

ANNIE: Oh is that why you sent a mob in to ransack the British embassy?

TAZ: We did no such thing.

ANNIE: They gutted the place. Burnt the Union Jack, ripped down a portrait of Her Majesty the Queen for God's sake!

TAZ: The Queen was Victoria. And the people were justly angry about Iran's treatment. A hundred and eighty people and entities had sanctions slapped on them. Punitive measures against our banks, against our transport sectors against our energy sectors...

ANNIE: Because you're not complying with the inspectors.

TAZ: We let the IAEA in.

ANNIE: Yes after an awful lot of hullabaloo.

TAZ: And their findings were inconclusive by your own admission.

ANNIE: But they did uncover a steel chamber at Parchin used for testing explosive components for a nuclear weapon. The size of a bus. That's why we had to impose sanctions.

TAZ: And do you know who these sanctions are hurting?

ANNIE: Look...

TAZ: Ordinary, working Iranians, that's who.

ANNIE: There have to be consequences.

TAZ: Oh, like civilian planes crashing on a regular basis because Boeing won't supply essential parts? Innocent people dying. You mean those consequences?

ANNIE: Consequences for breaking the terms of the Non-Proliferation Treaty.

TAZ: Iran has not violated the NPT.

ANNIE: Smuggling fissile material in through Turkey and Russia? Building a detonator factory at Fordow...?

TAZ: No because this...hang on...

TAZ suddenly starts frantically rifling through some papers.

ANNIE: What?

TAZ: ...wait let me...stop a minute. This is important.

MERCER: What is it?

ANNIE: Stop?

TAZ: Sorry but this is...I want to show you something.

MERCER: I'd prefer you to keep going.

TAZ: Shit, I can't find it. The NPT, the wording, I was re-reading it this morning.

MERCER: If these simulations are going to work we really need to stay focused.

TAZ: I must have left it...I just want to show you...I won't be two seconds.

ANNIE: Taz.

TAZ exits.

MERCER: What was that about?

ANNIE: He's frazzled. We all are.

MERCER: *(After a slight beat.)* I need to ask you a question.

ANNIE: I think I know what it is.

MERCER: You *know* him. Rather better than most. You've been working with him on this all these months.

ANNIE: You want to know if he's up to this.

MERCER: I mean he seems to have gone native.

ANNIE: Well he's been trying to get inside their heads. That's why he's so good on the details, on the arguments.

MERCER: But it's like he's tearing himself apart.

ANNIE: He lives and breathes the job. He has too. We all do.

MERCER: Yes but he mustn't allow himself to be compromised. We so desperately need to make progress this time. We can't just be met with a...a wall of denial. We have to break through it, smash though it.

ANNIE: With what. Taz was right, the inspectors report isn't conclusive.

MERCER: Then we need something else. A wrecking ball. Something that allows us to counter every obfuscation, every avoidance tactic.

ANNIE: That won't be easy.

MERCER: None of this is easy. For a start no one can agree on sanctions. Just this morning the French proposed a ban on crude oil imports, but the Greeks are worried they'll take a hit.

ANNIE: Even if they did agree without Russia and China we might as well give them a hundred lines.
'I must not build a nuclear bomb.'

MERCER: Well Russia and China are not at all convinced sanctions are a good idea.

ANNIE: Sure, because they want to keep selling them things.

MERCER: Meanwhile the Americans want progress at any cost.

ANNIE: Yes but what progress?

MERCER: Who the hell knows? All I know is we're on their turf. So we can't leave this party empty handed. That's why I need you to stay in Taz's face in these simulations. Be brutal. Make sure there's nowhere to hide. We have to pin these buggers down.

ANNIE: Fine, I can do that, but the Iranians are privy to the same intel we are. They know what we're coming at them with and they know how to deflect it.

MERCER: Then we need to work harder. Go beyond what we know.

ANNIE: How?

MERCER: That's your job. Use your imagination.

ANNIE: My imagination? I work for the EU.

TAZ comes back in the room holding a document.

TAZ: Got it.

TAZ slams the document on the table.

TAZ: The Nuclear Non-Proliferation Treaty. Here. Article two;

MERCER: Taz...

TAZ: Just a second...here...it says 'each non-nuclear weapon state undertakes not to manufacture or otherwise acquire nuclear weapons...'

ANNIE: Where are you going with this?

TAZ: But...article four states; 'nothing in the treaty shall be interpreted as affecting the inalienable right of all the Parties to the Treaty to develop research, production and use of nuclear energy for peaceful purposes.'

MERCER: For peaceful purposes being the key phrase.

TAZ: Yes and it goes on to say; 'All parties to the treaty have the right to participate in the fullest possible exchange of equipment, materials and scientific and technological information for the peaceful uses of nuclear energy.'

MERCER: Again peaceful purposes.

TAZ: But how do you prove their nuclear development is not peaceful? The only way of censuring Iran under the terms of the NPT is to prove their nuclear development is aggressive. For that they'd have to *do* something aggressive. Attack someone with a nuclear bomb.

ANNIE: When that happens it'll be time to go home. The talking will be over.

TAZ: But do you see what I'm saying? The Treaty, the way it's worded, it's contradictory.

MERCER: Oh great. That's just what we need.

TAZ: The point is whatever the inspectors say about hard water plants or detonator factories, or whatever else, we don't know for sure Iran wants an aggressive nuclear capability.

ANNIE: What about Ahmadinejad's threats to wipe Israel off the map? It's not the language of peacemakers is it?

TAZ: No, but he doesn't say he'll use a nuke.

MERCER: That's a subtle distinction the Israelis are in no mood to make.

TAZ: Look, I'm just saying, this is not clear-cut.

ANNIE: But that's exactly what Iran's banking on…this uncertainty over what to do? Their whole agenda is to keep everyone locked in this dance. Go round and round…because the longer it goes on the bigger the cracks get. It's Mao Zedong's strategy of Talk Talk Fight Fight. Keep negotiating even though you have no interest in coming to a settlement. It's a distraction exercise and we're falling for it. The only thing that's sure is the longer we keep talking, the longer nothing physically happens to stop them, the longer the Iranians have to build the bomb.

TAZ: So what are you saying? Send in the battleships? The F-16s?

ANNIE: Why not? Show we've still got the stomach if it comes to it. Show there'll be real consequences if they carry on defying the world.

MERCER: Annie...

ANNIE: Seriously. Why not threaten force?

TAZ: Cos it's the one way to unite the Iranians against us. They already feel surrounded by hostile enemies...Saudis calling for invasion, Wahabi-ists in Pakistan, Israel leaking attack plans. Why d'you think they want the bloody thing in the first place?

ANNIE: Well don't mind me I'm just trying to stop a nuclear war!

TAZ: And I'm not?!

MERCER: All right you two enough. Let's take a break. I need some air.

MERCER exits.

Silence.

ANNIE: ...look if you're not up to this we can ask Mercer if she'll replace you.

TAZ: Excuse me?

ANNIE: I mean if you think it's too difficult for you.

TAZ: Not up to this?

ANNIE: You're all over the place Taz. Breaking off the simulation...obsessing about the details of the NPT...

TAZ: You don't think details are important?

ANNIE: Yes, but you should be focusing on the negotiating techniques.

TAZ: I don't believe this.

ANNIE: Jalili's a heavyweight. He'll duck and weave…he'll have you tangled up in your own semantics and then he'll flatten you. I've seen him do it. And to better men than you. *(Firmly.)* I just want to make sure you remember whose side you're on.

Silence.

TAZ: I get these updates on my Blackberry…these news updates…and there was a story this morning about this British soldier in Afghanistan who…there was this Afghan boy, ten years old, and he was running errands in the camp…and this solider…well he'd been on the vodka the night before and he was pretty hacked off and hung-over and for no apparent reason he stabbed this kid in the stomach.

ANNIE: Taz…

TAZ: With his bayonet.

ANNIE: Look…

TAZ: On my Blackberry I'm reading this. Stabbed this kid for no reason. And it made me think you know, we've developed this…all this…technology…such extraordinary technology and we keep developing it. Every day we can do more and more amazing things. But we're just as savage as we ever were. Deep down.

ANNIE: That's not an argument for everyone having the bomb…

TAZ: That's an argument for no one having it. But that's not the world we're living in.

ANNIE: So why shouldn't the Iranians have it, is that it? Everyone else does.

TAZ: Exactly. And there hasn't been a war yet.

Are they really any more barbarous than us? Any less rational? We tolerated Russia having them. China, Pakistan. North Korea, why not Iran?

ANNIE: Because Iran going nuclear would be a catastrophe. It'd be viral. Israel'll shoot off a warning shot, the Saudis'll have to start building the bomb, so will Kuwait, so will Syria, Jordan, on and on... At the same time the US'll move her subs into The Strait of Hormuz to deter an attack on Israel, which'll make Pakistan show its teeth, which'll make India nervous. The Russians'll mobilise their nukes making China jittery, making North Korea flex its muscles...it's a tinderbox. You think Iran won't strike the match if she can?

CULLOCH: So how long do you think we've got?

CULLOCH, a man in a sober suit stands at the door. It's hard to know how long he's been there, but certainly TAZ and ANNIE didn't notice him come in.

ANNIE: Excuse me?

CULLOCH: Before they go nuclear. How long?

ANNIE: Sorry but this is a private conversation.

CULLOCH: Didn't sound private.

TAZ: D'you mind me asking who you are?

CULLOCH: You're with the EU delegation right?

TAZ: That's right.

CULLOCH: Carter Culloch. I was looking for Baroness Mercer.

ANNIE: She's not here.

CULLOCH: No, I see that, but it is pretty important I speak with her.

TAZ: Who did you say you were again?

ANNIE: I bet he's CIA.

TAZ: Why do you say that?

ANNIE: Look at the way he's dressed.

TAZ: She thinks you're CIA.

CULLOCH: She's right.

TAZ: Oh. Right.

CULLOCH: So? What's the answer? How long? Ball park.

ANNIE: An Iranian bomb? A year to manufacture enough
Highly Enriched Uranium…two or three make a
deliverable weapon.

CULLOCH: So we're talking about a window here of what…a
few years?

TAZ: Hang on. A window?

CULLOCH: Yeah the timeline between now and when Iran has
a nuke. Problem?

TAZ: Where do I start?

ANNIE: Taz…

TAZ: First. Just a second. First what you said implies an
immovable certainty on your part.

CULLOCH: It does?

TAZ: So is that your position? You have no doubts at all that
the Iranians are developing a nuclear weapon?

CULLOCH: Have you read the latest IAEA report?

TAZ: I have and there's nothing definitive in it about Iran's
nuclear ambitions.

CULLOCH: Really?

TAZ: A lot of conjecture, a lot of speculation…

CULLOCH: I didn't catch your name.

TAZ: Humble. I'm an independent analyst. I've been brought in by Lady Mercer to assist on these negotiations.

CULLOCH: Hubble? Like the telescope?

TAZ: Humble. Taz Humble.

CULLOCH: Oh. Thought it was Hubble.

TAZ: Look…

CULLOCH: You ever heard of a man called Dr. Ali Al-Hashemi?

There is a lighting change as AL-HASHEMI enters to denote this is happening in a different time and place. He sits at a table. ANNIE and TAZ do not interact with HASHEMI, but CULLOCH should move between scenes with fluidity.

ANNIE: I have. He was Chief Engineer at Natanz?

TAZ: What about him?

CULLOCH: I've been debriefing him for the last twenty-three hours.

ANNIE: He's here? He's in New York?

CULLOCH: He was on his way to a conference on Particle Physics in Antalya…he got word through Turkey he wanted to defect. They got word to us.

ANNIE: And what's he saying? Has he got something that would affect the negotiations?

HASHEMI: I had a banana smoothie and an eggplant gyro. The boy went to the deli on the corner.

CULLOCH: That boy is a highly trained Navy Seal. You're a significant asset.

HASHEMI: It was a very fine sandwich. Very fine indeed. But why so much food? They stuff the bread so you can't get your jaw around it.

CULLOCH: Doctor Hashemi, I'm Carter Culloch. I'm here to debrief you.

HASHEMI: And what did you have Mr. Culloch?

CULLOCH: Excuse me?

HASHEMI: For lunch?

CULLOCH: Chinese take out. Can we get on with this? We've got a lot to get through.

HASHEMI: Oh I wanted to thank you for putting the television in my room. I watched this man on the CNN. Piers Morgan I believe he was called. He was talking about the danger of an Iranian bomb. He had some very strong views I must say.

CULLOCH: Did he?

HASHEMI: Yes. I thought he must be an expert in the fields of particle physics and geopolitics to be so confident on this subject.

CULLOCH: I don't think he is.

HASHEMI: Well. I googled him. I discovered his qualification. He was a judge on your *America's Got Talent*.

CULLOCH: Don't watch it.

HASHEMI: Nor me. I prefer *The Real Housewives of Orange County*.

CULLOCH: OK, look, can we just…

HASHEMI: But I believe the President is a fan. The Ayatollah prefers *Judge Judy*.

CULLOCH: Are you yanking my chain or what?

HASHEMI smiles.

HASHEMI: I have to admire you Americans. You make news entertainment and entertainment you make news. It's how you control the narrative. How you anaesthetize the world into submission. And you accuse us of using soft power.

CULLOCH: We're not here to talk about American popular culture.

HASHEMI: Why not, it's everywhere. Your music. Your films.

CULLOCH: What's your point?

HASHEMI: That *we* understand you better than *you* understand us. Know your enemy Mr. Culloch. We understand your sensibility because we are surrounded by it. Until you people wake up, until you engage with my country it will always have that advantage over you.

Beat.

CULLOCH: You led us to believe you had some information we might find of interest.

HASHEMI: You could say that yes.

CULLOCH: Care to share it?

HASHEMI: I can confirm we are developing a nuclear bomb.

Stunned silence.

TAZ: He's admitting it.

CULLOCH: He says they never stopped weaponising. Just covered it up.

ANNIE: Talk talk fight fight.

CULLOCH: Excuse me?

TAZ: Chairman Mao.

ANNIE: This is what they do.

TAZ: Their negotiators are in the air as we speak. If they are developing a bomb they'll break the terms of the NPT. The UN Security Council will have to censure them.

CULLOCH: The UN? Please. It'll be us. We'll have to go in.

TAZ: Go in?

CULLOCH: But this time the intel has to be watertight. A hundred per cent. We can't have another Iraq.

ANNIE: So if you're not a hundred per cent why tell us?

CULLOCH: Call it a new spirit of sharing.

ANNIE: You mean you wanted to use us to test the Iranians. See if they implicate themselves.

TAZ: You think they sent him? You think he's a Trojan Horse?

CULLOCH: They know we're giving money to North Korea.

ANNIE: Plus if we believe they're building a bomb it shows the sanctions aren't working.

TAZ: There's somehting else. You said he was working at Natanz.

CULLOCH: What about it?

TAZ: Well isn't it... *(Gets a file and looks through it.)* Yes... satellite photos...and they don't show heavy water reactors, or the production of HEU.

ANNIE: So what?

TAZ: Natanz is designed to hold centrifuges to produce low enriched uranium...twenty per cent max. Not the ninety per cent HEU you'd need for a bomb.

CULLOCH: Yeah I asked him about that?

ANNIE: What did he say?

HASHEMI: They built a tunnel...under the plant. When our work at Isfahan was detected, they moved it to Natanz. Built the tunnel. That way we could avoid spy planes watching our work.

ANNIE: So is this guy for real or is he full of horse shit?

CULLOCH: Good question.

Blackout.

When the lights come up, ANNIE and TAZ are gone. CULLOCH looms over HASHEMI.

CULLOCH: And what were you working on there? In this tunnel under Natanz?

HASHEMI: We were trying to convert yellowcake into uranium hexafluoride. We had been trying to convert it into uranium tetrafluoride so it could be fed as a gas through the centrifuges. And then convert UF4 into UF6. But it is a perilous process because the UF4 is tainted with an oxyfluoride impurity which might condense and block the valves.

CULLOCH: Are you succeeding?

HASHEMI: Close. In spite of that Israeli computer worm that shut down a fifth of our centrifuges. In spite of losing some of my best people.

CULLOCH: Oh so I see this is why you are here. Worried you might be next on Mossad's hit list, so you've come here with this yarn? You've seen what happens to the others. You think defecting will save you from getting your face blown off while you're brushing your teeth.

HASHEMI: I am telling the truth!

CULLOCH: See, I've been reading your file. *(Pulls out a dossier.)* Born in the town of Shahr-e-Kord in central Iran. Moved to Tehran as a teenager just as the Iran/Iraq war broke out. Two of your brothers died in the fighting. Your sister died when the Iraqis carpet bombed your town. Must have eaten you up. Festered. That kind of tragedy.

HASHEMI: That was a long time ago. Another lifetime.

CULLOCH: Yeah but I bet it made you crazy. All these outsiders rejecting your Peoples' Revolution, screwing with your country, trying to control it. Is that why they sent you here? To screw with us back?

HASHEMI: Why who sent me? Nobody sent me.

CULLOCH: Did you believe it would make the US treat you better? Cos they feared you. Cos what you learned from all these American books and these American movies is we respect one thing. Strength. The power to destroy.

HASHEMI: You fear us already. Bomb or no bomb.

CULLOCH: *(After a slight pause.)* You studied Political Theory at Cairo University before getting your doctorate in Particle Physics in Kings College in London. Why d'you change course?

HASHEMI: It's not so unusual. My father was a chemist. He always wanted me to follow him into science.

CULLOCH: After London you joined a team working on uranium conversion at Isfahan nuclear reactor. You were then transferred to the Natanz Plant where you conducted nuclear weaponising-relevant activities involving neutron initiators, triggering systems, implosion experiments and God knows what else. Trust the Brits to educate the most senior bomb maker in Iran.

HASHEMI: Your flippancy betrays you Mr. Culloch. You can't hide your anxiety.

CULLOCH: Yes I'm anxious. Can you blame me? With those medieval nut-jobs who run your country. All their talk of the Shi'ite Messiah and the end of days...

HASHEMI: The people who talk about end of days are those lunatic Christians in Texas. One of whom was in the White House. So don't talk to me about end of days. That's your philosophy not ours.

CULLOCH: So Iran doesn't back suicide bombings? In Syria, Lebanon, Israel...

HASHEMI: You are the hypocrites. You shower Saudi princes with money, support corrupt Pakistani generals. Why are they so deserving of your affection and not us?

CULLOCH: You seem angry.

HASHEMI: Yes I'm angry. Wouldn't you be? Wouldn't you be sick...of...of being loathed and manipulated by the most powerful country in the world?

CULLOCH: You don't play ball. It's the price you pay.

HASHEMI: We are not unruly children to be kept in line Mr. Culloch. We have a history of civilisation that makes the West look embryonic. The Achaemenid Empire ruled from the Balkans to North Africa for four thousand years they ruled, the...the Seleucids and the Parthians and Sassanids for another thousand after that, we are not mischievous teenagers to be controlled and contained. That is why I am angry.

CULLOCH: Then why would you help us?

HASHEMI: But I am not helping you. I am doing what I must do to save my country.

CULLOCH: Or are you saving yourself?

HASHEMI: You think it costs me nothing to come here? To reach out to my enemy? You think my family is not in danger every moment I am here? I have three daughters.

CULLOCH: See I found it curious that you started as a politics major so I did some more digging. You've also got political ambitions. It's pretty underground, yes, but still.

HASHEMI: I have attended some meetings so what?

CULLOCH: Oh it's more than that. You're a key player.

HASHEMI: You think this is politicking?

CULLOCH: Cut the head off the snake. And put your team in charge. Is that it?

HASHEMI: And what if that team was a moderate pro-Western one?

CULLOCH: That would be fantastic, except I'd have to ask. Why now?

HASHEMI: It has to be now. The whole Middle East is crying out for change. My country should be leading this change; economically, politically, morally…not sinking deeper into isolation…no…no it must be now. This regime must be removed.

CULLOCH: Regime change?

HASHEMI: Yes. By all means necessary. The Americans must support an uprising.

CULLOCH: So this is why you're here?

HASHEMI: We need money, we need tanks, guns, air support. It's the only way.

CULLOCH: Support your movement? Put you and your friends in power?

HASHEMI: You will bitterly regret it if you don't.

CULLOCH: But I thought it's because you were developing a bomb.

HASHEMI: …What?

CULLOCH: Wouldn't that be why you've chosen now to speak?

HASHEMI: Well yes, yes I have but…

CULLOCH: But it also conveniently coincides with the Arab Spring?

HASHEMI: These people will have the bomb. These nut jobs as you call them.

CULLOCH: You think we can just go crashing in all guns blazing, because some guy turns up and says there are weapon-making facilities buried in tunnels?

HASHEMI: Isn't that your usual modus operandi?

CULLOCH: If we go to war on a flimsy pretext and find no nuclear weapons…

HASHEMI: I have the computer models. The data, the drawings, the photographs…

CULLOCH: Inconclusive. You could have cooked them up. You have the capability.

HASHEMI: I cannot afford to bluff. Not when everything I hold dear is at stake.

CULLOCH: I need to know why now. I need to know why you've chosen this moment to come forward. I need the truth from you now.

Pause.

HASHEMI: How much do you know about Quantum Theory Mr. Culloch?

CULLOCH: Excuse me?

HASHEMI: Quantum Theory. How much do you know?

CULLOCH: I majored in French Existentialism at college.

HASHEMI: Ah then you're perfectly placed to save the world from nuclear Armageddon.

CULLOCH: I know about Shrödinger's cat.

HASHEMI: Oh yes?

CULLOCH: Something about a dead cat in a box.

HASHEMI: You put a cat in a box with a phial of poison precariously balanced so it might break open. You shut the box…after a while…

CULLOCH: Right, the cat could be dead from the poison or alive.

HASHEMI: Two possibilities existing at the same moment.

CULLOCH: But only one truth, right? The cat is alive or dead. Just because it's hidden from view...

HASHEMI: But the point is to accept the uncertainty. To hold the two possibilities in your head at the same time.

CULLOCH: OK I understand the theory so what?

HASHEMI: I'm not sure you do. I suspect you have a neurotic need to impose certainty on the situation. You Americans fear chaos. You think it is bad for business. So you try to impose order everywhere. American apple pie order. But you cannot impose order on the Middle East. Chaos is its natural state. Like sub-atomic particles, when a force is exerted on them, they behave unpredictably. The Iranians have no problem with this. They accept uncertainty. They can co-exist with it. This is why they are winning.

Blackout.

When the lights come up CULLOCH is sitting in the same position, but now MERCER has replaced HASHEMI opposite him.

MERCER: The US isn't seriously contemplating military action?

CULLOCH: Hashemi has political ambitions, sure, but if he is to be believed, what's the alternative?

MERCER: Let diplomacy do its job.

ANNIE: I say we confront them. We accuse them of breaking the terms of the NPT. We threaten them with a UN Security Council censure. Tough sanctions even from Russia and China. The threat of military intervention...

MERCER: No...

ANNIE: These people are laughing at us.

MERCER: And what if he's lying?

TAZ: I say we keep talking. There are still ideas that haven't been tried. A multinational consortium to oversee the enrichment programme, an interlocking system of force declarations, data exchanges…an open skies agreement…

ANNIE: It's all containment. It doesn't *solve* anything.

MERCER: But containment's all we have.

CULLOCH: Your government doesn't agree with you. They're deploying subs to the Gulf. Armed with Tomahawks.

MERCER: I'm sure that's precautionary.

CULLOCH: Things have changed since your Embassy got trashed. You've got skin in the game now.

MERCER: I'm sure our people can restrain themselves in spite of that.

CULLOCH: You Brits. Still got that superior attitude, even now.

MERCER: Much as I'd like I can't take credit for the actions of Her Majesty's government, I work for the EU. There's a distinct and growing difference.

CULLOCH: Yeah but you're still one of them.

MERCER: I'm an Englishwoman if that's what you mean.

CULLOCH: You still think if we just smooth things over, keep everything nice and civil, everything'll turn out rosy, but your snooty manner just makes everyone pissed.

MERCER: And America's been dazzlingly constructive in this particular area.

CULLOCH: At least we act. At least we go and get stuff done. All you guys do is talk.

MERCER: We call it diplomacy. You Yanks should try it one day.

CULLOCH: Well the US Congress is getting skittish. And if the President thinks there's no other way of curbing Iran's nuclear ambitions he'll have no choice but to send in the fifth fleet.

MERCER: And I have to stress again...that would be another monumental error.

CULLOCH: OK...look...you're running these negotiations. I've told you what I know. If you think it'll make the slightest difference...keep talking.

CULLOCH turns to go.

MERCER: Mr. Culloch. You've met this man. Is he bluffing?

CULLOCH: I'd be guessing.

MERCER: Isn't that all we can do? Guess.

CULLOCH: *(To himself.)* Shrödinger's cat.

MERCER: Sorry?

CULLOCH: Nothing. You have a great day.

ANNIE: So what now?

CULLOCH goes. Pause.

MERCER: I have to meet the Under-Secretary General for Economic and Social Affairs. Something about an international conflict that's brewing over fish. I'll be back in an hour. Let me see what you have.

MERCER goes.

ANNIE and TAZ give each other a look and get back to the table. Silence.

TAZ: Last year I was working on this report to the Trilateral Commission...East Asia and the International System I think it was. And at the end we had this big...this big blowout. Dinner, a bar, a club. And I got really leathered, you know, and I...I met this woman.

ANNIE: Oh God...really? You're doing this now?

TAZ: And I was...you know...dancing with her...I was giving her my best moves...you know, we were really hitting it off.

ANNIE: You gave her your best moves, how could any woman resist?

TAZ: Well I think she was pretty hammered herself. Oh don't get me wrong she was hot. And she had this...she fixed you with this stare, you know, she had a real intensity... like she sucked in life.

ANNIE: You always did go for the unhinged ones.

TAZ: And before I know where I am she asks me back to hers.

ANNIE: D'you really think this is the appropriate time for one of your war stories?

TAZ: So we're messing about on the bed...you know... canoodling...and she breaks off to go to the toilet. So OK, I think, I'll take in the moment. You know. How often d'you get a chance to just relish the moment? To go...I'm alive here. I'm doing this. And I lean back on the pillow and I feel this lump...this hard lump under the pillow. And I reach under and there's this...axe.

ANNIE: An axe?

TAZ: She's got this fucking hand axe under the pillow.

ANNIE: Don't tell me you stayed?

TAZ: Well I couldn't concentrate on the job in hand. My eye just kept going over to the pillow as we were you know...

ANNIE: Canoodling.

TAZ: Canoodling. Yes. Eventually I made my excuses and left.

ANNIE: Jesus...

TAZ: And at first I was horrified you know...but then I thought fair enough, she's picking up strange men in bars. She wants to protect herself.

ANNIE: So you didn't do anything about it?

TAZ: She's not going to use it. It's just there to make her feel safe.

ANNIE: Either that or one day some poor fucker will end up with a hand axe in his skull.

TAZ: …Yeah. She was a bit unpredictable. Could go either way.

ANNIE: Shall we get on with this?

TAZ: Sure.

Blackout.

End of play.

THE LETTER OF LAST RESORT
by David Greig

First production
The Tricycle Theatre, London, 16th February 2012

Characters / Cast

PRIME MINISTER	Belinda Lang
JOHN	Simon Chandler
Director	*Nicolas Kent*

Setting
After the next election.

It's late.

She writes, or rather attempts to write.

He enters.

...

Still here?

...

Burning the midnight oil.

...

Getting the old legs under the desk.

...

Not old legs. Of course.

...

Young legs.

...

New legs at any rate.

Is there something?

Something?

I'm rather in the middle of –

Of course.

Didn't someone say?

Say?

The young man I asked him to screen.

He said you were busy.

Still.

I thought I'd pop by.

It is your first day.

Right.

Just wanted to check everything was all right.

Everything?

Arrangements, rooms, people.

Arrangements are fine, thank you.

I just wanted to check that you were on top of things.

– sorry your name is – ?

John.

And you are?

Arrangements.

Well, John – I think I'm pretty much – of course it's all new
– I mean I'm still getting lost in the corridors and so on –
and arrangements are – unfamiliar shall we say – but yes
– I think that – yes – essentially I think I'm on top of things
so far – so far – anyway.

Good.

…

*It can be…discombobulating. Especially on the first day. The
realisation that one is…in charge. Holding the reins. It can
unnerve one.*

One is fine. One's nerve is holding.

One feels quite comfortable holding the reins.

Good.

So, if there's nothing else.

As a matter of fact, there is something else,

Right.

Just a small matter, it'll barely take a moment, but nevertheless, it is a key part of arrangements. If you don't mind?

Can it wait?

Given that I'm here.

How key?

Quite key.

A moment?

A couple of moments.

May I finish this first?

Of course.

It's just – this is – I wouldn't mind getting it out of the way – if that's all right.

She writes, or rather attempts to write.

...

What is it. The... (A gesture.) ?

A letter of condolence.

Oh.

Yes.

Would you rather be alone?

It's fine.

I could go out into the corridor?

It's fine just –

With the young man.

No –

Yes, I'll just...

Just…

Hover.

She writes, or rather attempts to write.

…

Do you need – ?

It's fine.

She screws up the paper and throws it away.

There is a template.

I don't want to follow the template.

No.

This young man – soldier – a boy – let's call him what he is – a seventeen-year-old boy – and he's – he's – anyway – it's my responsibility – I represent – to write – to the mother – to write – not a template – my personal – if I start using templates now then what else? – no – you have to confront – one has to confront – I have to confront these things – however difficult.

I understand.

However difficult it is for me to write – it's not as difficult as –

Being dead.

Reading it – the mother.

Oh. Yes. I suppose.

It's my responsibility to be honest, to be human…

Start as you mean to go on.

She writes, or rather attempts to write.

It's hopeless.

She screws up paper and throws it away.

I wish to express my…

As a mother I feel…

– it's cheap. It's…

…

You reach out a hand – you hold a hand.

…

Silence is the only honest response.

…

Still – to offer no acknowledgement – no letter – that would be worse.

Yes.

And there is a template.

She takes a new blank sheet.
She looks at it.

…

Perhaps a break.

You're right. I can't do this now. I'll come to it later. My head's – *(Gesture.)*

All right – so – what time is it? –

A few minutes to twelve.

– so – John – the small key matter?

Yes.

What is it?

We need you to write a letter.

Right.

The letter of last resort.

The letter of last resort.

It shouldn't take a moment.

All right.

It's usually done on the first day.

No problem.

She takes another sheet of blank paper.

John?

Yes Prime Minister?

What is the letter of last resort?

Ah.

Fill me in.

Well, as you know Prime Minister, at any given moment there is always at least one British Trident submarine on patrol somewhere in the world. Its mission being to avoid detection and remain hidden. Inside each Trident submarine is a safe, and inside that safe is another safe and inside that safe is an unopened letter. That letter contains your orders in the event that the captain of the submarine believes that the United Kingdom has suffered a devastating and decapitating nuclear attack.

'Letter' because it's a letter and last resort because it's only ever opened in the event that – and this would have to be ascertained after the Captain and Vice Captain had completed a number of very specific protocols – the Captain believes that the United Kingdom has been attacked, London has been destroyed, all the members of the government killed, defence installations obliterated and so forth.

...

Once again – given the execution of these long and complex protocols – if the Captain determines that the United Kingdom no longer has functioning political or social networks sufficient to give him a legitimate order then…

He opens the safe?

He opens the safe.

And then he opens the other safe.

Yes.

And then he opens the letter.

That's correct.

And the letter says.

Well that's very much up to you Prime Minister.

…

You may wish to tell him his orders are to fire our nuclear missiles in retaliation or you may wish to tell him his orders are to refrain from retaliating.

…

The letter is the means by which we ensure that, even in the very last resort, the correct democratically elected hand remains on our nuclear trigger.

Even if the correct democratically elected hand has been vaporised.

Yes.

And democracy vaporised with it.

Quite.

It's a key matter for you to attend to because – in order to preserve secrecy the previous letters were destroyed this morning when your predecessor left office and so – at the moment – as a nation – were anything untoward to happen – not that we expect it to happen of course but if it it were to happen – in the absence of a letter – we would be – so to speak – 'caught with our pants down.'

...

Is there a template?

No.

How does the captain of the submarine know who he's retaliating against?

Responsibility for a massive decapitating nuclear strike is not something that it would be easy to hide.

No.

Our captains are kept up to date with the latest geopolitical movements. They constantly monitor radio and satellite traffic – world broadcasting services and so on. There may even be, in the case of such a massive attack, a direct admission of responsibility on the part of the aggressor nation.

I see.

...

How does the captain know that there's nobody left?

He follows the protocols.

Protocols?

Signs.

What signs?

Not so much signs as the absence of signs.

Right.

No signal traffic on UK defence frequencies. No announcements by UK government or Royal officials. The absence of Radio Four.

The absence of Radio Four?

Yes.

The absence of Radio Four? Really?

Amongst other things.

She sings the theme tune of The Archers.

Ha ha.

Because without *The Archers* there is no civilisation.

In fact it's only one of a number of protocols and if you think about it – it makes a certain amount of sense given that if the BBC were in any way able to broadcast someone would be doing so…so the implication of its absence is relatively severe.

Sorry.

Really Prime Minister we just need you to write… From the PM…etc., etc…to Commander HMS etc, etc… Given the execution of protocol x and subject to validation procedure y by your Vice Commander your orders are to either a) retaliate in a like for like manner…or b) not retaliate or c) act on your own discretion or d) some other option.

There's another option?

You may wish neither to retaliate nor withhold retaliation but instead ask the commander to put the submarine at the disposal of Australia.

Right.

Or New Zealand.

Because they are part of the Commonwealth.

Yes.

…

Also they might be left.

Look, John – the thing is – this is all very well but it's – I don't – I mean it's all so hypothetical –

I don't catch your meaning, Prime Minister?

There isn't going to be a devastating nuclear attack on Britain. London isn't going to be wiped out by bombs from Russia or whoever… I don't know

Iran

Iran?

As a for instance.

Yes well… All right, Iran but the fact is the political conditions are just – it's impossible in the modern world. Maybe during the Cold War but nowadays it's…who would do it? Who would actually launch the missiles? Which leader of which country thinks an attack like that on a country like this would have any kind of…would have any meaning?

Still.

I could write a nursery rhyme on this piece of paper, John, it's never going to be read. The events that require it to be opened are quite simply impossible. They're never going to happen.

Except of course that they have happened.

What?

The events have happened.

No they haven't.

They have.

London has not been attacked, John.

With respect Prime Minister London has been destroyed.

Look – London – trees – sky – bird – cat – night.

The only circumstances in which this letter will be read are those in which there are no longer trees, or birds or cats…or London or you. As you write this letter you must assume a world not as it is now but a world as it exists in the circumstances of the letter's

reading. As soon as you put pen to paper, Prime Minister, London ceases to exist.

...

What did Fuckface write?

I'm sorry?

Monsieur Coiffeur?

I'm terribly sorry I don't –

My predecessor.

Oh. Him. I can't say.

Say.

I can't.

Do.

No.

A moment.

She writes.

Dear Commander – what name?

Vanguard, Victorious, Vigilant, Vengeance.

I want to use a name.

A name?

Jim, Stan, Jack, Reg.

The Protocol is to use the titular form e.g. Dear Commander HMS Vengeance.

Britain has been destroyed. John. The Queen is dead. London is ashes. This man's family are dead. Everything he has ever loved is gone. I want to use his name.

Peter, David, Hugh, John.

Dear Peter…

Dear Peter…

Where is he reading this?

In his cabin?

Where.

Under the sea.

Under the sea where – I'm just trying to picture it.

His location will be secret.

Roughly.

Nobody know where they patrol.

I bet Russian intelligence has a fair idea.

In fact not.

Nobody?

Nobody.

Don't they have sonar?

Once every three months a Trident submarine slides out of the Firth of Clyde and into the North Atlantic where they hide, usually under the polar ice, or in deep mid-ocean trenches, or in the shadow of undersea mountain ranges…they may receive communication but they send no communication out. Nuclear engines mean they move silently. Their only purpose, their entire mission whilst on patrol is to remain undiscovered so that in the event of a devastating and decapitating nuclear attack the United Kingdom still has the capacity to retaliate.

…

Unless of course your orders are that he not retaliate.

Look, no! I'm not going to do this John. I'm not going to write any letter. The truth is, I'm pretty ambivalent about the whole nuclear weapons thing anyway. It may be a fact of government but – no – Giving orders in advance is – no.

Ambivalent?

Yes.

That's not something about which I was advised.

It's not something I like to advertise but it's true. I was at Greenham John, and Faslane. Not as an actual protestor. As a – fellow traveller. I went with people. I was beside people. In the end I found it all too…marginal – somehow we're stuck with these things – these – but come on, ideally we'd be rid of them wouldn't we…first chance we got. Nobody **likes** nuclear weapons. Do they?

I do.

…

I like nuclear weapons very much.

You like the shape. The penis shape.

It's not their form I like. It's their concept.

You're military. The military always like weapons.

In fact, on the whole the military are rather against nuclear weapons.

Are they?

Military people like fighting wars and nuclear weapons are useless for fighting wars.

Nuclear weapons aren't intended to fight wars Prime Minister. They're intended to NOT fight wars. Their destruction is abstract and conceptual. They are truly philosophical weapons. The military, on the other hand, like weapons to be concrete and visceral.

Not you though.

No.

Even though you're military.

I'm not military, Prime Minister, I'm arrangements.

And arrangements likes its weapons philosophical?

The knife stabs, a gun fires, a pilot clicks a button and there is a vanishing puff of pixels and smoke but if the commander of a submarine launches a nuclear missile strike he instigates the total destruction of an entire society, millions of people die, vast tracts of land are poisoned forever – the death he brings isn't prosaic or literal it's philosophical. It's death as we would experience it ourselves – all-encompassing, personal, and yet at the same time utterly unimaginable.

And that's good?

It's the foundation of deterrence. In all the years of their existence, no nuclear armed nation has ever attacked another nuclear armed nation.

Until now.

I don't understand?

Birds – trees – cats – London

Oh… I see. Yes. No nuclear armed nation has ever attacked another nuclear armed nation…until now.

I'm dead?

Yes.

The captain is somewhere?

Yes.

We don't know where?

Yes.

In a cabin.

Yes.

At his desk? Does he have a desk?

Yes.

Not dissimilar to this desk?

Yes.

Let's role play.

Role play?

You be the captain, I'll be me.

What?

Just – imagine…

All right.

You open the safe and then you open the other safe and then…you see me and you say –

Madam, I have reason to believe there has been a completely devastating nuclear first strike on the United Kingdom. I am no longer receiving communication from any identifiable British sources. Monitoring of radio frequencies from other countries suggest that London has been destroyed along with Glasgow and therefore the submarine bases on The Clyde. I have gone through every one of the protocols designed to confirm the extent of the situation and each protocol has been passed. What are your orders?

What's your name, Captain?

My name isn't important Madam.

What is it?

John.

Hello John.

Hello Madam.

John, have you tried Radio Four?

I have tried Radio Four.

And?

White noise, madam.

Who did it, John?

...

...

China.

China?

China.

We've been expecting it madam.

I thought this was a surprise.

They've been threatening it but we didn't think they'd actually do it.

Where are your missiles targeted?

Beijing.

Peking?

Beijing is the correct term.

I think we can call it what we fucking like after what those fuckers have done to us.

Yes madam.

Is retaliation technically feasible?

We have two missiles on board with nuclear warheads. Targeting coordinates are programmed into the computer. If I turn the launchkey we will hit Beijing sorry Peking within twenty-five minutes.

The turn of a key.

Two keys, I operate the launch jointly with my second-in-command.

What's his name?

It really doesn't matter madam.

What's his name?

Kevin.

Do your crew know about this?

Not yet.

Who knows about it?

Only myself and – Kevin.

How many people will die?

Madam?

How many will die?

Probably something in the region of 10–15 million people, madam.

...

...

What went wrong.

I don't know madam.

China.

Yes.

They always seem so rational.

They must have believed an attack was in their interest.

Didn't they know we'd retaliate?

They must have calculated that we wouldn't.

Did we indicate we wouldn't retaliate?

Quite the opposite, madam. We forcefully indicated that we would.

But they didn't believe us.

No.

Why?

I'm not sure.

Not sure?

There is a possibility.

Which is.

It's possible that they believed it was in their interests to attack and that, despite our indication, after the attack we wouldn't retaliate –

Of course we're going to retaliate, why wouldn't we retaliate?

Because to retaliate would be irrational.

...

What's the point. Britain is already functionally destroyed. There is no state to speak of. Most of our people are dead. Whatever remains of our society is defeated.

I'm sorry but –

There may be an emotional argument in favour of a revenge attack but in all likelihood the Chinese cabinet ministers who ordered the attack will have long ago repaired to a well-defended nuclear bunker somewhere in remote Mongolia. Any retaliation we enact will be nothing less than the wholesale murder of fifteen million civilians and all to no political or military purpose.

They started it.

It may also be illegal. Under international law it's likely to be construed that the captain of the ship – me – who fires the retaliatory weapons could be committing a war crime.

That's a very fine argument isn't it?

It's actually a very central argument. I'm not sure I would be able to obey an order that effectively induced me to commit a war crime.

Your country is destroyed. All the people you love are dead.

I realise it's an emotional scenario.

It's an emotional fucking scenario all right. I don't see how there can possibly be a problem with international law. Surely – any putative court at any future time will understand that retaliation in the form of wiping out Pe-fucking-king is legitimate use of counter force to their massive provocation.

Yes, but you're not giving the orders in the future madam, you're giving the orders now.

So?

When you write the letter you're not in the heat of battle. You are in the cool of the present moment. And in that moment you are ordering the murder of twenty million innocent civilians in the full knowledge that it's an act with no military or political purpose. If and when you write that order, therefore, you are consciously committing a war crime.

I'm vapour. John. What are you going to do? Sue me?

You may be dead but I am alive.

Alive in a tub under the sea – a tin tub and a bomb, that's all that's left of Britain John, the United Kingdom, the British Empire, Albion – all that's left of all we ever were and have been is you and Kevin and some bewildered seamen in a can.

The moral point remains, madam.

...

I saw one once. We were on a hillside above Loch Long.
My boyfriend at the time was a protestor I went up for a
weekend to visit him. We were sitting round a campfire.
My bum wet with morning dew. Bacon frying. The forest
orange and brown, a whisper of mist. The loch still and
black and then suddenly I saw it – Trident – Cutting
through the water silent and black, like time passing.
Everyone started banging pots and pans. Booing. Yelling.
My boyfriend shouted 'murdering cunts!' 'murdering
cunts!' But I felt...warm. I was surprised. To see them,
the sailors on the deck, the captain on the tower. I felt
warmly towards them – them? – it? I didn't say anything,
of course. I hated nuclear weapons. Obviously. But there
was an ambivalence, the sailors on the deck, the movement
through the water, the seriousness of it. I felt as if I was
watching my father riding home on a black horse.

The boyfriend – he is – was he – vetted?

Long gone.

...

John is there really no way you can contact someone in
authority? Can't I order you to call, I don't know, the UN?

*Any form of radio contact would give away our position and
render us open to being sunk which would therefore remove the
potentiality of the weapon.*

Right. So I can't order retaliation because that would be a
war crime. So I must order you not to retaliate.

She takes a blank sheet of paper.

Dear John... Dear Kevin...if you're reading this then I can
assume there has been the most terrible fuck-up. I'm truly
sorry. However it came about you can be sure it was not
intended. Please don't retaliate. Whatever dignity there is

left in the British state we muster at this moment and we refuse to stoop to their level and commit a war crime. My orders are that you sail to Australia, if it still exists, and put yourself at the disposal of the Australian navy…accept the orders of their Government. I hope that in some way you and your crew manage to build a life of some worth out of the horror in which you find yourself at this moment. God Bless you all.

She signs.

Of course madam.

She puts the letter in an envelope.

Thank you John.

That was helpful.

You're welcome madam.

She offers him the letter.

Prime Minister –

Yes.

Could I offer some contrary advice?

What?

Some advice against ordering non-retaliation.

Are you Captain John now or Arrangements John?

Arrangements John.

Arrangements John, it's late.

I know but – as I say – this really is key.

All right.

Prime Minister, deterrence can really only work in principle if a potential aggressor nation has complete and utter certainty that in the event of a devastating decapitating first strike they will be retaliated against.

But – you just – you – we

If you don't commit to retaliation then the United Kingdom will always be vulnerable to the threat of an aggressive decapitating strike.

To retaliate is irrational.

That's as maybe but without the irrational threat of retaliation there is no point in having nuclear weapons at all.

John?

Yes, madam.

Are you saying that the entire edifice of Britain's nuclear weapons establishment, the submarines, the sailors, the missiles, the bases, the whole multi-billion pound programme…are you saying that in the end it all rests on what I write on this piece of paper now –

Yes, madam.

To write 'retaliate' is monstrous and irrational. To write 'don't retaliate' renders the whole nuclear project valueless.

Yes, madam.

So these words – these words which I have to conjure now in the face of unimaginable horror – a horror which I have to imagine – and if these words now exist – we must assume that in some way this unimaginably horrible world has come into being. Into this abyss – this – John – into this darkness that we are spared but which someone will have to confront in reality – into this darkness these words must go in that darkness they must say – 'don't retaliate' but the only logic I can use to write the words comes from the actual world in which I'm writing – the world of light – and in that world the only words I can write are 'do retaliate.'

Yes madam.

Which brings me to another paradox. If these words exist then I'm dead, and not just me but all those who would represent me. So these words, therefore, that I must conjure tonight in the form of orders, orders written, stamped, folded amongst the full pomp of power of state of 'arrangements' are in fact nothing but marks on a page that, on the moment of opening, will mean absolutely nothing...nothing. Why? Because who is going to enforce them? Who will make John obey my orders? Kevin? No – these impossible words that I write as orders are in fact not orders but a request – not even a request – a thought – barely even a thought...a prayer? A spell? – an incantation written by a little girl, spat on, sung over burned to ash then hidden in a locket and given to a boy before he goes to sea – I speak you a spell – spoke it – will speak it – and when you open the locket the spell is broken.

...

And so whatever dark magic it is that gives these words their power now will in the moment of opening be reversed but each syllable, each phoneme smeared across the paper will carry reverse magic – a dark anti-animation the opposite of life, the opposite of breath – death – the suck of death.

Yes.

Logically, I have to write 'retaliate'.

Yes.

She takes a blank sheet of paper.

Dear John, there's been a fuck-up – please retaliate.

Yes.

She signs the paper.

She puts it in an envelope.

She gives it to him.

Madam…

Yes John.

It isn't enough just to write it.

…

You have to mean it.

What?

If you don't mean it, your ambivalence will reveal itself in your behaviour. It will appear to our enemies that the letter of last resort does not order post-strike retaliation.

But it does. I just wrote it.

What you actually write doesn't matter. All that matters is what the world thinks you've written.

I could show them the letter.

The moment you show the world the letter you'll be potentially liable for prosecution for inciting a war crime.

What can I do then?

There really is only one rational thing you can do.

What's that?

Be irrational.

John it's late – I – what?

The rational thing for you to do Prime Minister, in all matters of world affairs, is to behave in a wayward and dangerous manner.

You can't be serious.

I'm deadly serious. In order to keep the value of a nation's nuclear deterrent the rest of the world has to believe that the leadership of that nation is basically – irrational – on a knife edge – ready to go off at any moment – likely to do berserk things – they have to look at that nation and believe that its premier is driven by enough psychopathy that they would be willing to see twenty million innocent civilians die for no other reason than sheer revenge.

Right.

It's called the 'crazy' strategy.

The crazy strategy.

It's a strategy which Israel pioneered. Iran has adopted it. America pursues it quite successfully.

What about us?

We on the other hand adopt a different strategy.

Our strategy is rather more subtle.

What is it?

The letter of last resort.

John – I don't understand – I can't –

Try Prime Minister,

my head's full –

Twenty million human lives depend on this.

Try.

A moment.

It's rational to behave irrationally.

Yes.

Therefore it's irrational to behave rationally.

Yes.

Therefore we prove our irrationality by behaving rationally.

Yes.

The more rationally we behave the more irrational we appear to be.

Yes.

So… We must pursue rationality to utterly insane levels.

Yes.

We pursue rationality until it creates a logical paradox so extreme that it breaks through the simple binary opposition of rational and irrational and it becomes something else – something beyond – something transcendent.

You've got it!

The letter of last resort.

The letter of last resort.

A letter which has to exist but which can't exist, a matter in which the only rational way to behave is to be irrational, writing words whose purpose is never to be read…absurd.

Isn't it!

Like an absurd drama.

Yes!

It's like an episode of *Yes, Prime Minister.*

Ha ha! Yes, Prime Minister.

An absurd scene in which You and I are caught up in one of the odd conundrums of British political bureacracy – mysterious and maddening but oddly endearing.

Quite!

Or

Pirandello.

Yes Pirandello.

But of course we aren't in a play by Pirandello.

No.

This scene is 'like' an absurdist drama but it's not actually an absurdist drama.

No.

Because I am the Prime Minister.

Yes.

And you're John.

Yes.

Except, of course I'm not the Prime Minister?

No.

Because I'm dead

Yes.

And so are you.

Yes.

A moment.

Prime Minister? Are you all right?

I can't help thinking of him, John, him and Kevin, under the sea, hanging in the shadow of a mountain searching the frequencies – no *Archers* – no *Today* programme – no *Gardener's Question Time* – no cricket – No *Woman's Hour* – no *Feedback* – no *Thought for the Day* – No voices at all – only the absence of things – he's searching but there's nothing there – only the empty wavebands calling out over the sea.

Shhhhh.

Shhhhh.

Prime Minister.

It is late.

We don't want to be caught with our pants down, so to speak.

No.

Would you mind writing the letter now.

She takes a blank sheet of paper.

She writes, or rather attempts to write.

He waits.

The End.

FROM ELSEWHERE: ON THE WATCH...
by Zinnie Harris

First production
The Tricycle Theatre, London, 16th February 2012

Characters / Cast

OTTO	Daniel Rabin
RUDOLF	Rick Warden
Director	*Nicolas Kent*

FROM ELSEWHERE: ON THE WATCH

Modern day. Iran.

We are outside a modern nuclear building.

OTTO and RUDOLF enter wearing radiation suits. They carry a huge amount of equipment.

It's extremely heavy and hard work.

They walk in and take their masks off.

OTTO: hot in there.

RUDOLF: yes.

OTTO: hotter than last year

RUDOLF: not sure.

OTTO: look on your chart
does it list temperature?

RUDOLF looks at his chart.

RUDOLF: yes

OTTO: then mark it down
it felt a little warmer

RUDOLF: I'm not sure it did

OTTO: it did

RUDOLF: did we take a reading?

OTTO: you've got the thermometer
I tell you I could feel it on my skin

RUDOLF: this is 2012, not 1940.
they ask for things a bit more precisely.
these days

OTTO: OK

RUDOLF: OK

RUDOLF looks at the chart.

RUDOLF: how much warmer?

OTTO: I'll go back in

RUDOLF: you'll have to get it cleared

OTTO: we were just in there –

RUDOLF: we had the official visit yes, but to go back in

OTTO: I'll get it cleared

RUDOLF: you'll have to see our friend

OTTO: I'll see our friend

RUDOLF: the Ayatollah's grandson

OTTO: if you believe him

RUDOLF: I believe him

OTTO: anyway I can handle him

Beat.

OTTO: I'm sure I'm not mistaken, I know it's a bother now

RUDOLF: I'm OK with it, if you want to mark it down any
   change after all

OTTO: we're talking about an important area after all

RUDOLF: we're talking about the workers' canteen

Beat.

RUDOLF: just so we are clear.

OTTO: I'll see our friend there, I'll get clearance

RUDOLF: he'll send you back to the hotel with a flea in your
   ear
   just so as you know.
   we've done it.

we've been in.

one hundred and seventeen committee hours to get us
access.

we've snooped around, what we've seen we've seen.

your hunch about the workers' canteen area

it'll have to stay as just a hunch.

OTTO: I'll mark it down

RUDOLF: you do that.

OTTO: could be they have something underneath.
something that we couldn't see on the satellite

RUDOLF: anything is possible
or the canteen air conditioning isn't working

OTTO: we've heard there's talk of a new tunnel
if they are building a new tunnel
undeclared

RUDOLF: of course they're building a tunnel
we all know they're building a tunnel
just where
that's the question
is it under the canteen, which personally despite your
hunch I think unlikely or
over there

OTTO: over there?

RUDOLF: the other side
did you see that door?

OTTO: which door?

RUDOLF: as we were going in
a door
wasn't there last year
whole load of cardboard boxes very nearly obscuring it
but nevertheless a door

OTTO: I saw the boxes

RUDOLF: you missed the door?

OTTO: are you sure it was a door?

RUDOLF: a door is a door, right?

> *Beat.*

OTTO: so you think the tunnel is on the other side…?

RUDOLF: I'm just saying there was a door.
> an *undeclared* door.
> why not declare a door.
> if it's just a door, why not stick it in the official report, say
> hey everyone we are building a door
> I mean of course it's not just a door, a door always leads to
> somewhere, yes?

OTTO: I can't believe I missed it

RUDOLF: they'd stacked up quite a few boxes

OTTO: just as we went in?

RUDOLF: yes

OTTO: damn
> have you marked it down?

RUDOLF: of course I have
> alongside the five buildings undeclared, the seventeen
> pieces of new equipment undeclared, the box of yellow
> powder origin unknown, the 24 tonnes of metal piping
> undeclared
> it's a joke really

OTTO: I think I should just nip back, take that temperature

RUDOLF: and anyway while we are here, we are looking here,
> North Korea is doing god knows what, Pakistan

OTTO: don't you think?

RUDOLF: if you want.

OTTO: why should it feel a bit warmer in the canteen?
    hot even
    just to be sure
    I could say I have left something

RUDOLF: you think?

OTTO: we were there just a second ago, I could just say I left
    something
    I can be bumbly and forgetful
    we're scientists after all
    terribly sorry, I just forgot something

RUDOLF: what though?

OTTO: I don't know help me

RUDOLF: it took one hundred and seventeen hours of
    committee time to get us in, for us to go in there in the first
    place you can't just 'nip'

OTTO: I left my glasses

RUDOLF: you don't wear them

OTTO: they don't need to know that
    I could say I left my glasses then when we don't find them,
    that's just an oh well

RUDOLF: you can try

OTTO: I think I should
    call it a hunch
    we are watch dogs after all, not ostriches

RUDOLF: are we?

OTTO goes off.

RUDOLF is left.

He takes out his glasses.

And his sheets of paper.

His sandwiches.

RUDOLF: is that what we are?

He bites into his sandwich.

RUDOLF: an ostrich
a watchdog
an auditor
a political exercise
a breaking pad
an apology
a ghost

OTTO comes back.

RUDOLF: no?

OTTO: no

RUDOLF: why not?

OTTO: the gates are all shut

RUDOLF: at half past three?

OTTO: no one there to ask

RUDOLF laughs.

OTTO: don't laugh

RUDOLF: you'll have to mark it down, as a hunch
possible raised temperature in the workers' canteen

OTTO: they're still there, of course
you can't shut down a nuclear reactor
they just aren't opening the gate

RUDOLF: of course not

OTTO: I could almost hear someone on the other side

RUDOLF: listen one hundred and seventeen committee hours
to get us through the door, we did what we had to.
we saw what we saw.
I'm not surprised they aren't letting us back in
If I were them I wouldn't either.
we know they are building a tunnel, and they know that we
know they are building a tunnel
the probability is they are only building a tunnel to distract
us from something else they are doing, something they
know but we don't know they are doing yet.
until it shows up on a satellite image bought from a spy
agency, and denied, and challenged and denied again and
more committee hours and then people like us sent back in
with a clipboard to do a counting exercise.
it's a game.
and in this game, you can't nip.
leave it to the politicians and mark it down.

OTTO: are you sure about that door?

RUDOLF: yes I am sure about that door.

Beat.

OTTO: your glasses have broken

RUDOLF: where?

OTTO: there you have a small crack

RUDOLF takes them off.

RUDOLF: damn look at that
they were made in Berlin

OTTO: a lifetime ago.

RUDOLF: still.

He puts them on.

OTTO: you look ridiculous

RUDOLF: thank you

OTTO: you'll have to get them fixed, before we deliver our
report

RUDOLF: out here?

OTTO: how did you break them anyway?

RUDOLF: I don't know
I wasn't observing them.
they broke I suppose of their own accord

OTTO: I suppose they did.

Beat.

OTTO: are you ready?

RUDOLF: pass it all over to the politicians you mean, let them
do their bit.

OTTO: that's what we are here for.

RUDOLF: in the hotel room last night, while you were having a
rest, I was on the internet.
I don't know why I typed my name into an internet search
engine.
I was just interested you know, great scientist, winner of
Enrico Fermi Award, the Compley Medal, author of three
books, a hundred papers, member of this committee, that
committee, professor, teacher, physicist
and you know what came up?
a picture of a mushroom cloud.
Rudolf Peierls.
and underneath a mushroom cloud.

OTTO: that's why we are here.

RUDOLF: we aren't here

OTTO: that's why it feels like we are here.

why we have to carry these bloody packs on our bags
every day.

RUDOLF: an apology?

OTTO: no, a counting job

RUDOLF: I want to go home.

OTTO: don't think about it.
    fill in the boxes, file the report
    we'll go home one day

RUDOLF: we were excited, we were young
    if we hadn't have told them what we knew

OTTO: we had to tell them what we knew.
    we've always agreed that, whatever happened after
    Iran, Korea, America, all this
    that was something else
    we had to tell them what we knew.
    it's up to them to control it now.

ANADYR'

by Elena Gremina
Translated from the Russian
by Sasha Dugdale

Characters / Cast

KHRUSHCHEV	
ALEKSEI	his assistant, aged 35
KHRUSHCHEV'S GRANDDAUGHTER	aged 6
VLADILEN SAVEL'EV	Naval Commander and Captain of Submarine B-55, aged 40
EGOR GARKUSHA	Major in the KGB, aged 40
ANTON ZVEREV	radio operator
FILIPP KOZLIKOV	former student of the Moscow State University, now a sailor aged 19

Sailors, Soldiers

Setting

The action takes place between 21st and 27th October 1962 at the dacha of KHRUSHCHEV, the General Secretary of the Soviet Communist Party, and on submarine B-55.

SCENE ONE

At KHRUSHCHEV's dacha. It is an ascetic environment. ALEKSEI, his assistant is demonstrating a new acquisition: a table lamp in the shape of a globe. When switched on, the globe lights up.

ALEKSEI: This is how it switches on, Comrade General Secretary. And here's how it switches off. Marvellous, isn't it. It was made at an armaments works but for wider consumer use. They're offering them to schools. This very first model is for you.

KHRUSHCHEV: Very original.

ALEKSEI: It's for you, Nikita Sergeevich, the people at the works asked it if could be given to you as a gift on the anniversary of the Great October Revolution.

KHRUSHCHEV: I can see you've taken a shine to it.

ALEKSEI: It will help school children and students. A visual aid. It's like the whole world in their hands.

KHRUSHCHEV: You like all this pointless excess, don't you? Original things are almost always pointless excess. An armament works making consumer goods! Well they've picked their time haven't they? And you've got new shoes on again! You're a communist, not a diplomat or an undercover spy. Why on earth do you need to look so smart?

ALEKSEI: *(About the globe.)* ...But Nikita Sergeevich, it's an ideologically sound object. See, the Socialist Countries glow pink and the USSR shines red.

KHRUSHCHEV: Red. *(He looks at the globe.)* Right and proper. The colour of the blood of the labouring classes.

ALEKSEI: Well, yes...

KHRUSHCHEV: Are you grinning? You've got a fine manner on you. Can't work out whether you're joking or not.

ALEKSEI: Nikita Sergeevich! My own father died in the war. How could I joke about something like that?

KHRUSHCHEV: Well that's something *they* just don't understand. This yellow bit, is this America?

ALEKSEI: And that green spot there, that's Cuba. The Isle of the Free.

KHRUSHCHEV: Turkey! Show me where they keep their missiles.

ALEKSEI: *(Showing him.)* Two in Izmir, one in Anatolia.

KHRUSHCHEV: *(Reddens, grows angry: he is reminded of his unpleasant thoughts.)* And where are ours? Well? Where are they? Our missiles? Point them out!

ALEKSEI: Nikita Sergeevich, I see this wasn't a good idea, this gift. You're right, they should stick to their basic military work.

KHRUSHCHEV: *(Seriously angry now.)* And how long does it take our missiles to reach New York? Well?

ALEKSEI: *(Frightened that KHRUSHCHEV might now explode with rage.)* But you know that, Comrade General Secretary.

KHRUSHCHEV: Tell me! Or have you forgotten how to speak in your fancy shoes?!

ALEKSEI: Our S-50 with a nuclear warhead takes 24 minutes to reach New York from our base in Vladivostok. But their missile from its Turkish base in Izmir takes 8 minutes to get to Moscow. Still that's just geography – what can you do? The Americans were just lucky they could do what they liked in Turkey. We haven't got that option.

KHRUSHCHEV: America's had all the luck for a very long time. And everyone's used to it. The whole world. You're my assistant and you stand there and tell me that if we have a nuclear war our missiles will take twenty minutes to reach New York and Washington and theirs will take ten minutes to reach Moscow and Leningrad. Eh? And how are we to take that, eh? What right have they got to threaten us?

ALEKSEI: Well there won't be a war, will there.

KHRISHCHEV: And what about if the Americans make good their threat of invading Cuba? We'll just sit around waiting to hear on the radio how they destroyed the Isle of the Free? Doesn't that worry you?

He looks appraisingly at ALEKSEI.

Why is your generation so different? You've taken your eye off the ball! And it's too soon for that! What America wants, America does. America wants to be even richer, even more powerful. They can never have enough. They want to rule the world. And the whole world lives by their say-so! And all because our missiles take 24 minutes and their Turkish missiles only take 8 minutes. Because our missiles have to travel further. It's unjust. Or is it all good and right? Would you like to be an American then?

ALEKSEI shakes his head in terror.

KHRUSHCHEV: America can cope with the injustice. They're used to being wealthy and strong. They have no idea what it's like to fight a war on their soil. They never lost 20 million in the war, and yet they're still playing at winners. That's just how they are. They've forgotten how to suffer. And they've become unjust. The only justice for America, is America. They don't understand other countries, countries where there is poverty, where the labouring classes suffer.

KHRUSHCHEV's granddaughter runs in, she sees the glowing globe and gasps. KHRUSHCHEV beckons her over.

KHRUSHCHEV: Look. Here's our homeland. See how big it is. The best people in the world live here. Because they've suffered so much and they deserve happiness. And that green spot there is Cuba. Those are our friends. We defend them.

GRANDDAUGHTER: Against who?

KHRUSHCHEV: There are people who want to hurt them, but we won't let them be hurt.

ALEKSEI: Can I go now?

KHRUSHCHEV: Write this down: Comrades! We need to find a way of answering the American threat and avoiding war. American missiles in Turkey are targeted at Moscow and Russian towns. I know how we can make the Americans respect us. It's impossible to do it with conventional weapons. All we have are the Gods of contemporary warfare – nuclear weapons. We'll put a hedgehog down America's trousers!

Darkness. In the darkness a little girl turns a lit-up globe, then that light too is put out.

SCENE TWO

Darkness. The splashing of waves and the sound of an engine. Submarine B-55 is rising to the surface. The signal lights are illuminated and people begin climbing one by one out of a hatch: GARKUSHA, the CAPTAIN and the radio operator ZVEREV. ZVEREV immediately begins trying to get a signal on the radio. Then others come out onto the deck. They are all completely exhausted, they gulp in the fresh air.

GARKUSHA: Stop! Stop that! No coming up to deck. Get back down below! Get back down –

CAPTAIN: *(To GARKUSHA.)* Who gave you the right to issue orders? *(To the SAILORS.)* Carry on, men.

The SAILORS come on deck. They breathe heavily.

CAPTAIN: Permission to get undressed, those who have eczema. Medical personnel, permission to carry out procedures in the open air.

The SAILORS undress and a medical officer shines a torch on the sailors' bodies and brushes a green disinfecting solution onto the outbreaks of eczema on their skin.

GARKUSHA: Until the radio operator gets a message, our instructions are that no one in the crew should come up onto the bridge.

CAPTAIN: They need to breathe some fresh air. And the ones with eczema need the air on their skin. It's about forty degrees down there in the hull, down in the main quarters it's sixty degrees.

GARKUSHA: I told you you needed to regulate the temperature better.

CAPTAIN: Regulate the temperature? How? We're in the Sargasso! It's like floating in hot soup. What do you think the water temperature is? This is an arctic submarine and for some reason we've been sent to the Sargasso Sea!

GARKUSHA: Are you trying to debate the orders we've been given? I'll say it one more time: no one in the crew should come onto the bridge until our signaler has had a message.

CAPTAIN: Keep you hair on. Your message is going to be in code anyway. *(With irony.)* Or do you think there's a spy aboard just waiting to decode your message and pass it on to the enemy?

GARKUSHA: I don't see anything funny about it. You make lame jokes, Captain. They used to know how to deal with jokers like you – ten years in a labour camp, and sometimes worse. Eh, Comrade Commander?

CAPTAIN: Oh yes, the KGB isn't what it used to be… Believe me, you lot aren't a patch on what they used to be. Experts. Broke an arm with one blow at interrogations.

GARKUSHA: *(Mildly)* Well indeed, you're right there.

ZVEREV: *(To GARKUSHA.)* Comrade Garkusha. Permission to speak. There's no message yet. We're still waiting.

CAPTAIN: At ease, man. *(To GARKUSHA.)* Why the hell is he reporting to *you* on *my* boat? You're a civilian.

GARKUSHA: I am not permitted to give my rank.

CAPTAIN: Well then you're a civilian. So stop giving orders.

GARKUSHA: And you stop upsetting yourself over silly things, Comrade Commander. We're on the same mission here. Oh, and by the way. Which of you is Kozlov?

FILIPP KOZLOV steps forward and straightens up.

GARKUSHA: Kozlov, I have been informed that you are breaking rules. You have been putting toilet paper into the toilet after use, and on this tour you have been instructed to burn it in a special incinerator, so no potential enemy can trace our whereabouts.

CAPTAIN: *(With irony.)* You've been getting some valuable information, haven't you… Who's putting toilet paper in the toilet…

GARKUSHA wants to answer but a radio signal sounds.

ZVEREV: I've received a message, sir, and I'll begin decoding now.

GARKUSHA: Seaman Kozlov. I'll have a little talk with you later and we can discuss your lack of vigilance then. *(To the CAPTAIN.)* Comrade Commander we've received our message, so issue orders to submerge the boat. We could be seen from the air.

CAPTAIN: At night?

GARKUSHA: They have night vision.

CAPTAIN: So they see us. So what? What's the secret?

GARKUSHA: Give the order and you'll get a full explanation later.

CAPTAIN: Long overdue. *(To the SUBMARINERS.)* Clear the bridge. Prepare to dive.

The SAILORS climb back into the hatch.

CAPTAIN: *(To GARKUSHA.)* Listen here. If I gave the order it was only because I didn't want to challenge your authority in front of the crew, your authority as an officer...as a... But... Really... The toilet paper stuff... It's just ridiculous. What's the great secret?!

GARKUSHA: Why haven't you ordered the dive?

CAPTAIN: Come off it! How come you know *my* boat's destination and yet it's hidden from me? You really take liberties. What right have you got to issue commands to my crew?

GARKUSHA: You've got an ill-disciplined crew, Comrade Commander. Have you ever read the file on that Kozlov? Do you know why he was thrown out of college? Listening to *Voice of America* in his student hostel. Enemy radio! That's what your crew is like! I'll be doing some work on him.

CAPTAIN: First things first. Why don't I know where we are going? What's this big mystery about? So even the commander of a submarine doesn't know where his boat is heading.

GARKUSHA: Why haven't you ordered the dive?

ZVEREV: *(Coming over.)* Comrade Garkusha, permission to speak. The message is decoded.

ZVEREV hands over the decoded message to GARKUSHA, but the CAPTAIN seizes it and reads.

CAPTAIN: All this is is permission to open the third envelope. It's bloody ridiculous. The first envelope was opened in the Bosphorus, the second in the Strait of Gibraltar with orders to sail towards the Sargasso Sea. So what's in the third envelope? And the fourth?

GARKUSHA gets the envelope out of a concealed pocket and offers it to the CAPTAIN. The CAPTAIN opens it.

GARKUSHA: Just don't forget that I allowed you to open the third envelope yourself.

CAPTAIN: *(Opens the envelope and reads.)* ...Stealthily and at top speed to Cuba. We're going to Cuba? Why the hell Cuba? And what's in the fourth and last envelope then? I demand you open it now. This is all ridiculous.

GARKUSHA: Three things I have to say to you. It is not ridiculous. That's the first. Secondly –

CAPTAIN: Stealth and top speed, I mean, that alone's nonsense. Underwater we can't do more than three knots, and if we're on the surface we can't be stealthy.

GARKUSHA: ...Secondly the KGB hasn't changed. It's the same under Khrushchev as it was under Stalin, and you'll get to test that out on your own skin Comrade Commander, if you continue this sabotage.

CAPTAIN: Be careful what you say, Comrade!

GARKUSHA: And thirdly, and most importantly. This submarine must dive! We're only supposed to come up to the surface to receive radio messages. You read your orders: We should be travelling with stealth – and here we are hanging around on the surface and we could be seen at any moment. From the sky and from the sea.

CAPTAIN: We haven't finished taking in air.

GARKUSHA: *(Doesn't understand.)* What air?

CAPTAIN: For goodness sake you're like a child. Didn't they explain to you what a submarine was? That a diesel submarine needs to come up to surface to recharge? What on earth did they tell you?

GARKUSHA: *(Stunned.)* This isn't a nuclear submarine?

CAPTAIN: Of course it isn't. It's a diesel, and it needs time to recharge its battery. We can't dive just yet.

GARKUSHA: *(In shock.)* They told us these were nuclear submarines.

CAPTAIN: Well now… I did hear that they sent out a nuclear submarine but it broke down and came back to base. And anyway you wouldn't get a nuke to go anywhere secretly – Have you ever heard what a noise they make?

GARKUSHA: But you have got nuclear missiles on board?

CAPTAIN: They call the nukes bellowing cows, because they made such a racket. You can hear them miles away.

GARKUSHA: Have you got nuclear missiles on board?

CAPTAIN: Yes but that doesn't make us a nuke. B-55 is a diesel boat. It has a nuclear warhead on its torpedo. We were told this was a training voyage, so we could get used to our new weapons. *(He looks at GARKUSHA questioningly.)* Was that true?

ZVEREV: Comrade Commander permission to report – I'm picking up plane radar, signal strength three.

CAPTAIN: What strength is the signal?

ZVEREV: Signal strength three.

GARKUSHA: What does that mean?

The noise of an aeroplane coming closer.

CAPTAIN: No – I think you need to tell *me* what it means…

The sound of an exploding device. A yellow light flares up.

GARKUSHA: Are we being bombed?

CAPTAIN: It's just a flare. They're marking where we are with the yellow light.

Another explosion, and another pillar of yellow light.

GARKUSHA: We were told that nuclear submarines would go to Cuba stealthily and at speed, protecting our ships with their nuclear missiles. No one told us they would need to come up to recharge their batteries.

CAPTAIN: *(Reading the instructions once again.)* Cuba? Our ships are carrying nuclear weapons to Cuba? And we're covering them? On submarines that need to come up every day to recharge? So is this war, then?

GARKUSHA: This is operation Anadyr'. So those are just warning flares? What are they going to do next?

CAPTAIN: Clear the bridge. Diving Stations. Take her down…

The thunder of a bomb. Darkness.

SCENE THREE

KHRUSHCHEV's study at his dacha.

ALEKSEI is reporting to him. KHRUSHCHEV is listening to his report. The globe-light flashes on and off. KHRUSHCHEV flicking the switch back and forwards.

ALEKSEI: I see you like your gift, Comrade General Secretary.

KHRUSHCHEV: One can always get used to excess. Are those new shoes you're wearing?

ALEKSEI: I have the most recent news on Operation Anadyr'.

KHRUSHCHEV: *(Referring to globe.)* So show me where Anadyr' is?

ALEKSEI: In the far North. The main town of the Chukotka Region.

KHRUSHCHEV: *(Looking at the globe.)* What a large country this is. So huge and trusting. How hard it is to defend it. '*Look at me, lying here in front of you! Come and hurt me!'* And our enemies are only too happy to kick us! They're just waiting for the right moment!

ALEKSEI: But we're ready to show them.

KHRUSCHEV: You didn't answer – are those new shoes again? How many pairs of shoes have you got?

ALEKSEI: Really, Comrade General Secretary! They're the same shoes. It's the trousers that are new. The old ones were worn through. My wife was at a congress of laboring women in the Socialist Brotherland Yugoslavia and she brought them back.

KHRUSHCHEV: Instead of wifely obedience, your wife brings you trousers from abroad! Eh? And anyway why does your wife have to go abroad? Surely there are plenty of worthy working women who aren't related to my staff? *(Turning red with anger.)* Why do I have to explain things like this to you? The Imperialists I can always target my missiles at, but what am I going to do with you lot?

ALKEKSEI is fearful that another fit of the famous KHRUSHCHEV rage is on its way and attempts to change the direction of the conversation gradually.

ALEKSEI: On the matter of the missiles. You wanted for a report on Operation Anadyr'. And here it is: Operation Anadyr'. You requested nuclear weapons and military force to be transferred to Cuba. To defend our brothers in the republic of the free from possible aggression by the United States. After our missiles have been delivered to Cuba, instant attacks can be made on the potential enemy's most important tactical sites at a signal from Moscow. Forty long-range missile launching sites are being set up with a reach of between 2000 and 4500 kilometres. Each missile carries a nuclear warhead and that means, Comrade General Secretary, that we are ready to answer the Americans.

KHRUSHCHEV: We are ready to stand up for peace. Peace is very dear to us, because unlike the Americans we know what war on our own soil is like. War for them is merely dropping bombs from a safe distance. But we know the price of war.

ALEKSEI: Should I note that down?

KHRUSHCHEV: No need. I can always remember that. *(He turns the globe.)* So New York is a mere 8 minutes for one of our missiles.

ALEKSEI: Quite right.

KHRUSHCHEV: We won't start it. Everyone knows we don't want a war. We couldn't want a war. We lost twenty million in the war.

KHRUSHCHEV flicks the globe-lamp's switch and the globe flashes and dies.

KHRUSHCHEV: Bulb's gone.

ALEKSEI: I'll get it mended, Comrade General Secretary. It's only the prototype after all. Our comrades at the works will make some changes and sort it out.

KHRUSHCHEV: That's no excuse. The whole country is a prototype *(Raising his voice.)* I remember how Kennedy looked at me. The son of a millionaire, and I'm the son of a miner, a factory fitter, and he despised me, although he hid it. We gave power to the people, the poor, we're the first in the whole history of man to build a new and just world, and all the imperialists are watching us, waiting for us to fuck up.

ALEKSEI: It won't happen. Our fleet is moving towards the coast of Cuba with nuclear weapons, ready to be deployed against a potential enemy. And four submarines fitted with torpedoes are on standby to protect the fleet from the possible aggression of our potential enemy.

KHRUSHCHEV: Nuclear torpedoes?

ALEKSEI: *(Looks at his papers.)* Each submarine is fitted with at least one torpedo with a powerful nuclear warhead. Yes. The submarines are under the command of experienced commanders and they are crossing the Sargasso Sea stealthily and at high speed.

KHRUSHCHEV: Are they nuclear submarines, as I was told?

ALEKSEI: *(Looks at his papers, frowns momentarily, but afraid of KHRUSHCHEV's rage, he continues glibly.)* That's absolutely right! Nuclear submarines. A new type of submarine that doesn't need to surface to recharge but can travel stealthily and at high speed.

KHRUSHCHEV: Well… *(Satisfied.)* New York, Atlanta. Washington? Eight or nine minutes and… But we won't start it.

ALEKSEI: Only if absolutely necessary.

The telephone rings.

KHRUSHCHEV: Get it.

ALEKSEI picks up the receiver.

ALEKSEI: Speaking. *(He listens.)* I don't understand. Can you repeat that? *(He listens in silence.)*

KHRUSHCHEV: What is it?

ALEKSEI: Nikita Sergeevich. Comrade General Secretary. The Cuban Air Defence Forces have shot down an American plane. A spy plan, a U2 flew over Cuba and…

KHRUSHCHEV: An American pilot?

ALEKSEI shrugs in amazement.

KHRUSHCHEV: Our hot-headed Cuban Comrades.

ALEKSEI: Perhaps Comrade Fidel can't wait and he's trying to speed things up.

KHRUSHCHEV: I want an emergency meeting. Will the Americans respond? Could they hit our boats? Good thing the fleet is protected by these nuclear submarines.

SCENE FOUR

Darkness. The B-55 is deep in the sea. From time to time the sound of signaling depth charges falling.

GARKUSHA'S VOICE: *(With a hint of hysteria.)* What the hell's going on. Why's the light gone? Are we sinking?

CAPTAIN: Turn on the emergency lighting.

SAILOR'S VOICE: It's not working. The battery's damaged.

CAPTAIN: Turn on the reserve battery. How much power have we got?

A weak light goes on. The inside of the B-55 appears. GARKUSHA is attempting to open a hatch.

GARKUSHA: Are we sinking? Are we sinking? How much oxygen is there left?

CAPTIAN: You need to put some iodine on your face, you've got eczema.

GARKUSHA: Why won't this hatch open!

CAPTAIN: You've got eczema on your face, and you're having a panic attack. All perfectly normal.

GARKUSHA: Open the hatch.

CAPTAIN: And what did you think would happen? You'd be sitting pretty firing your torpedoes at the Americans?

GARKUSHA: There's no point in getting angry with me. I didn't know any more than you did. I thought this was going to be a safe journey on a nuclear submarine. Like in Jules Verne's *20000 Leagues Under the Sea*.

CAPTAIN: A safe journey for you, killing others with nuclear torpedoes. Don't you like a fair fight? Do you know what those are? Signaling depth charges. They're trying to find us. And when they've found us they'll chuck a depth bomb down at us. Do you know what that is? Not much like Jules Verne.

GARKUSHA: Let me out! Please!

CAPTAIN: Petrov.

PETROV the medical orderly appears.

CAPTAIN: Carry out medical procedures. Comrade Garkusha has eczema as well.

PETROV: Yes, Comrade Commander.

He goes to GARKUSHA and paints his face with the green iodine solution.

GARKUSHA: Are you making fun of me?!

CAPTAIN: Skin afflictions are the result of the high temperatures, and of course the air in the submarine is full of bacteria. It's all quite normal. You just need a bit of sun on your skin when you get there.

GARKUSHA: We never will get there!

The explosion of a depth charge. The B-55 shakes.

PETROV: Turn round Comrade, you've got a bit of eczema here. *(Dreamily.)* I'm going to eat stewed fruit when I get back.

GARKUSHA: What? What are you talking about? Stewed what?

PETROV: Cherries. Stewed cherries, We have it for dessert sometimes. Half a cup.

GARKUSHA: *(Sobbing.)* This is terrible... Are we going to surface...

CAPTAIN: One of the hydroplanes is damaged. But we can surface. One last time. We can't submerge safely though after that.

PETROV: A jar of stewed cherries between the four of us. Nothing else a soul needs in this heat... And there's nothing tastier in the whole world...

He smiles at GARKUSHA who remains silent. His panic grows in him. Another signaling charge explodes. Everything vibrates.

GARKUSHA: They're bombing us! *(Muttering.)* Christ what's going on, Christ, Christ…

CAPTAIN: Yes they know where we are. Have you got any instructions to follow in this situation?

GARKUSHA: Christ… *(Disjointedly.)* Mother… I will come home, I promised…

CAPTAIN: Right now we need you. You've got the instructions.

GARKUSHA sobbing, attempts to open the hatch.

CAPTAIN: I see. Well, I don't think there's any point waiting for instructions.

The ORDERLY and the CAPTAIN seize GARKUSHA and wrap him in a towel. The ORDERLY gets out a syringe and injects GARKUSHA in the arm. GARKUSHA goes limp.

CAPTAIN: Officer! Stand by to surface.

ORDERLY: *(Cradling the sedated GARKUSHA and talking dreamily.)* Nothing nicer than sour cherries in their own juice in the whole world. I'll buy a crate of it when I get home and have it every day until I can't eat another drop. When I get home…

The sound of a bomb exploding. The lights go off. Darkness.

SCENE FIVE

KENNEDY's office.

ASSISTANT: *(Reporting to KENNEDY.)* We've managed to cut off a Soviet submarine. We believe the submarine to be damaged. It's manoeuvring with difficulty. Its hydroplane may be damaged.

KENNEDY: I was told Khruschev had a parcel sent for me?

ASSISTANT: Mr President, the Essex aircraft carrier wants permission to attack the Russian submarine if the commander won't give in to our demands.

A second ASSISTANT hands over the parcel. KENNEDY opens it. It is a record.

KENNEDY: A record? What the hell? Instead of a telegram?

(To the ASSISTANT.) I heard. Sink their submarine. But what will *they* do next then?

ASSISTANT: We need to attack the submarine before it can launch its missile.

The ASSISTANT puts the record on the record player. It plays the song 'Do the Russians want a war'.

KENNEDY: What's that?

ASSISTANT: *(Translates.)* Do the Russians want a war? Ask the silence? Ask the soldiers lying in the birch groves and their sons will answer. Do the Russians want a war! Ask the ones who fought, who embraced us at the Elbe, ask the mothers, ask my wife, and then you'll understand: do the Russians… do the Russians…

KHRUSHCHEV appears (this is in KENNEDY's imagination).

KHRUSHCHEV: Mr President. We can never want war. We support peace initiatives. All our equipment is defensive. Look at your missiles in Turkey. Why can't we do the same as you? We assure you, Mr President, we will not be the first to use nuclear weapons.

KENNEDY: *(Lifting the needle of the player abruptly so that there is a scratching sound. KHRUSHCHEV disappears.)* Bastard. The same old bastard. Can't believe a word he says. *(Looking at his ASSISTANT.)* Accompany the submarine into port when it surfaces. Any sign of defiance use force. Prepare my address to the nation. Put military readiness up to DEFCON three.

Darkness.

SCENE SIX – BRIGHT SUNSHINE

The submarine has surfaced. Sailors come out one by one onto the bridge, exhausted, half-naked, covered in green iodine solution. ZVEREV immediately begins attempting to make radio contact. A US dinghy appears not far off. An American orchestra is playing boogie-woogie.

CAPTAIN: I want continuous contact. I want to know what we should be doing. The hydroplane is damaged. Tell them if we submerge again we never come back up.

ZVEREV: There's no signal. The antenna is damaged.

LOUDSPEAKER: This is the Captain of the Essex.

CAPTAIN: *(Through loudspeaker.)* I can hear you. This is Commander Savelev, Captain of submarine B-55. *(Quietly to KOZLOV.)* Seaman Kozlov! What got you thrown out of college Kozlov?

KOZLOV: What are you going to do with me?

CAPTAIN: I don't give a damn what you did wrong, I just want you to tune this radio and find out if we're at war.

LOUDSPEAKER: Your submarine is surrounded. If you submerge or make any unadvised manoeuvres then a depth charge will be dropped on your submarine.

KOZLOV: There's no signal.

CAPTAIN: *(Shakes GARKUSHA who wakes from his sedated sleep.)* Come round will you… Give me your fourth envelope…

GARKUSHA: *(Raving quietly.)* I never came to visit you, not even on your birthday, forgive me mother…

CAPTAIN: Where's this envelope? *(Searches him, finds the envelope and opens it.)* Do you know what's written here?

GARKUSHA: All I've got left is my mother… My father died in the war, my uncle went to prison…never put that down in my files… I never came to see you… Not even to help cut wood or to clear the snow from outside her hut…

CAPTAIN: It says we have to reach Cuba at any price. What do you say to that Comrade Garkusha? Have you got anything to say? Any price – what price is that, then?

LOUDSPEAKER: You have five minutes. If you ignore this ultimatum your submarine will be destroyed. I remind you – we are outside all territorial waters.

KOZLOV: I've got a signal! It's American radio… Their President is speaking…

KENNEDY: Good evening, my fellow citizens:

This Government, as promised, has maintained the closest surveillance of the Soviet military build-up on the island of Cuba. Within the past week, unmistakable evidence has established the fact that a series of offensive missile sites is now in preparation on that imprisoned island. The purpose of these bases can be none other than to provide a nuclear strike capability against the Western hemisphere…

CAPTAIN: What? What's he saying?

KOZLOV: He's speaking very fast. I can't understand. I barely learnt the language… I was expelled from college too soon…

KENNEDY: In that sense, missiles in Cuba add to an already clear and present danger…this secret, swift, extraordinary build-up of Communist missiles…in violation of Soviet assurances, and in defiance of American and hemispheric policy – this sudden, clandestine decision to station strategic weapons for the first time outside of Soviet soil – is a deliberately provocative and unjustified change in the status quo which cannot be accepted by this country…

CAPTAIN: Translate it. Is it war then? War?

KENNEDY: It shall be the policy of this nation to regard any nuclear missile launched from Cuba against any nation in the Western hemisphere as an attack by the Soviet Union on the United States, requiring a full retaliatory response upon the Soviet Union.

KOZLOV: It's not war yet. But it sounds like they're about to start a war. And it sounds like they're starting with us. What is all this? Us stuck here in the sea? What's going to happen to us? No one's rushing to defend us are they? A full retaliatory response on the Soviet Union...

CAPTAIN: What else is he saying?

KOZLOV: Thank you and goodnight, he's saying. And that the military is on standby alert. Here, you listen...

But all of a sudden Russian can be heard on the radio.

VOICE: Anadyr' – can you hear me? Commander Savelev! *(The radio hisses and dies.)*

LOUDSPEAKER: Your five minutes is up. We know your hydroplane is damaged. We will escort you to port and you will live. But if you choose not to...

CAPTAIN: Standby to dive, officer. If we're lucky we'll get through their perimeter and disappear into their shadows. Standby.

LOUDSPEAKER: We will open fire.

KOZLOV: And if we're not lucky?

GARKUSHA: *(Smiling and talking to himself.)* ...Help clear the snow in the yard. So much snow in the winter, it comes right up to the windows... I promise...

The sound of firing. Darkness. Waves splashing.

VOICE: Anadyr'! Can you hear me? The situation has stabilized. The crisis is over. Do not carry out instructions... Can you hear me? Anadyr'? Anadyr'?

The End.

BIOGRAPHIES

Zinnie Harris is a playwright, screenwriter and theatre director. Her plays include *The Wheel* (National Theatre of Scotland, 2011), winner of the Amnesty International Freedom of Expression Award and a Fringe First Award; *The Panel* part of 'Women, Power & Politics' (Tricycle Theatre, 2010); *The Garden* (Traverse Theatre, 2010); *Fall* (Traverse Theatre, 2008); *Julie* (National Theatre of Scotland, 2006); *Midwinter* and *Solstice* (both Royal Shakespeare Company, 2004, 2005); *Nightingale and Chase* (Royal Court, 2001); *Further Than The Furthest Thing* (Royal National Theatre/Tron Theatre and then British Council tour to South Africa, 2000/1), winner of the Peggy Ramsay Playwrigting Award, John Whiting Award and Fringe First Award; *By Many Wounds* (Hampstead Theatre, 1999). She also wrote a new version of *A Doll's House* for the Donmar Warehouse in 2010. She has written two 90 minute dramas for Channel 4 – *Born With Two Mothers* and *Richard Is My Boyfriend* and several episodes for the BBC One Drama Series *Spooks*. Her directing work includes *While You Lie* (Traverse Theatre); *Julie* (National Theatre of Scotland); *Solstice, Widwinter* (both RSC); *Gilt* (7:84), *Dealer's Choice* (Tron Theatre Company); *Master of the House* (BBC Radio Four) and *Cracked* (2001 Edinburgh Fringe First Award). She was Writer-in-Residence at the RSC from 2000-2001.

Ron Hutchinson was Writer-in-Residence at the Royal Shakespeare Company and has had plays performed at the Royal National Theatre, the Royal Court Theatre, the Goodman, the Public Theatre, the Mark Taper Forum and the Old Globe. His plays include: *Topless Mum* and *Moonlight and Magnolias* (both performed at the Tricycle Theatre 2007/2008), *Says I Says He* and *Rat in the Skull* and adaptations of Mikhail Bulgakov's *Flight* and *The Master and Margarita*. A winner of the John Whiting Award and other awards, including the Dramatists' Circle Award, he is an Emmy-winning feature and television writer whose credits include: *Murderers Among Us, The Simon Wiesenthal Story, The Josephine Baker Story, The Burning Season, The Ten Commandments* and *Traffic*. He lives and works in Los Angeles and teaches screenwriting at the American Film Institute.

Lee Blessing's Pulitzer Prize-nominated *A Walk in the Woods* was performed last autumn at the Tricycle Theatre. Prior to this, his play *Wood for the Fire* was part of the Tricycle's season 'The Great Game: Afghanistan' in 2010, which went on a USA tour to Washington, Minneapolis, Berkeley and New York, and, in February 2011, played two command performances in Washington for the Pentagon. Blessing's other writing credits include *Eleemosynary*, which earned him a 1997 Los Angeles Drama Critics' Circle Award for Best Writing and garnered three others for production, direction, and lead performance. Blessing has written other works for stage, film, and television and has won numerous awards including: the American Theatre Critics Award, the Great American Play Award, and the George and Elisabeth Marton Award. Three of his plays have also been cited in *Time* magazine's list of the year's 10 best plays. His script *Cooperstown* was made into a film that aired on Turner Network Television and, in 1993, won Blessing the Humanitas Prize and three nominations for Cable Ace Awards. His most recent works include: *Lonesome Hollow* (2006) and *Great Falls* (2008), *When We Go Upon The Sea* (2009) and *A View of the Mountains* (2011).

Blessing heads the graduate playwriting programme at Mason Gross School of the Arts, Rutgers University.

Amit Gupta is a writer and director for stage and screen. His debut feature film, *Resistance*, adapted from Owen Sheers' novel, and starring Andrea Riseborough, Tom Wlaschiha, Iwan Rheon and Michael Sheen, opened in cinemas across the UK in November 2011. His follow-up feature, *Jadoo* – which he will also write and direct – is in pre-production and will shoot in March 2012. Amit's last play was *Campaign* – part of 'The Great Game: Afghanistan' (US tour) at the Tricycle Theatre.

Amit is developing a television series, *Dirty Law*, for Channel 4, with Lydia Adetunji and Jim Manos Jr. Amit is a member of the Tricycle's Bloomberg Playwrights Group.

John Donnelly's plays include: *Bone* (Royal Court Theatre); *Poll Tax Riots* (the Factory/Hampstead Theatre); *Corporate Rock* (nabokov/Latitude Festival); *Conversation #1* (the Factory/V&A/Latitude Festival/SGP); *Showtime* (LAMDA); *The Kraken Falls in Llangollen* (Clwyd Theatr Cymru/Write to Rock); *Songs of Grace and Redemption* (Liminal Theatre/Theatre503); *Alarms and Distress* (Redbridge Drama Centre); *Encourage the Others* (Almeida Projects); and *The Knowledge* (Bush Theatre). John is a past winner of both the PMA Award for Best New Writer and the NSDF Sunday Times Playwriting Award. He is currently a visiting lecturer at Central School of Speech and Drama and is working on a new commission for the Royal Court Theatre.

The Knowledge, *Bone* and *Songs of Grace and Redemption* are all published by Faber.

Colin Teevan's recent stage work includes: *The Lion of Kabul* part of 'The Great Game' (Tricycle Theatre); *How Many Miles to Basra?* (Winner of 2007 Clarion Award for Best New Play); *The Bee* and *The Diver* (Soho Theatre and NodaMap), both co-written with Hideki Noda; *Missing Persons, Four Tragedies and Roy Keane* and *Monkey!* (The Young Vic); *The Walls* (National Theatre). Adaptations include: *Kafka's Monkey* (Young Vic); *Peer Gynt* (National Theatre Scotland and Barbican Theatre); *Don Quixote* with Pablo Ley and *Švejk* (Gate Theatre/TFANA, New York). Translations include: Euripides' *Bacchai* (National Theatre) and Manfridi's *Cuckoos* (Gate/Barbican), both directed by Sir Peter Hall; *Marathon* by Edoardo Erba (Gate) and *Iph...After Euripides* (Lyric, Belfast). Television includes: *Single-Handed* for RTÉ and ITV; *Vera* for ITV; and forthcoming trilogy for RTÉ and Touchpaper TV. Colin has written over 20 plays for BBC Radio and is currently Senior Lecturer in creative writing at Birkbeck College, University of London. All his work is published by Oberon Books.

Diana Son is the author of the plays *Stop Kiss, Satellites, Boy, Raw ('Cause I'm a Woman)* and others. *Stop Kiss* and *Satellites* premiered at the Public Theater in NYC. *Stop Kiss* won the GLAAD Media Award for Best New York Production and was on the Top 10 Plays lists of *The New York Times, New York Newsday, The Daily News* and other major publications. Diana also won the Berilla Kerr Award for Playwriting. *Stop Kiss* has been produced at hundreds of theatres nationally and abroad, including the Soho Theatre in London.

Diana has been the recipient of an NEA/TCG residency grant at the Mark Taper Forum in Los Angeles and a Brooks Atkinson fellowship at the National Theatre in London. She has taught playwriting at NYU's Department of Dramatic Writing, Yale School of Drama and led a playwriting workshop for caregivers of the disabled.

Diana is currently co-executive producer of the upcoming CBS TV series *The 22* and has been a writer/producer for the series *Blue Bloods, Southland, Law & Order: Criminal Intent* and *The Westwing*. She has also written a number of TV pilots for CBS and A&E, a television movie for Showtime, and feature films for Fine Line and Robert Greenwald Productions. She is a member of the Writer's Guild of America, East; the Dramatists Guild, Women in Theatre and is an alumnus of New Dramatists.

She lives in Brooklyn with her husband and three sons.

Ryan Craig is Writer-in-Residence at the National Theatre Studio. He has written for television, film, radio and theatre. In 2005, he received a Most Promising Playwright Nomination at the Evening Standard Awards for his play *What We Did to Weinstein* (Menier Chocolate Factory).

Other plays include: *The Holy Rosenbergs* and the English version of Tadeusz Słobodzianek's *Our Class* (National Theatre); *The Glass Room* (Hampstead Theatre); *Broken Road* (Edinburgh – Fringe First Award); *Happy Savages* (Lyric Studio/Underbelly); and a translation of *Portugal* (National Theatre).

Television work includes: the Channel 4 drama documentary *Saddam's Tribe*, and episodes of *Robin Hood, Hustle* and *Waterloo Road* (BBC).

In 2005, he was Writer-in-Residence at BBC radio drama and his radio plays include: *English in Afghanistan, The Lysistrata Project, Hold My Breath, Portugal, The Great Pursuit* and *Looking for Danny*.

David Greig's award-winning work includes *The Strange Undoing of Prudencia Hart* (Tron Theatre, National Theatre of Scotland); *Midsummer* (Traverse Theatre and Soho Theatre/Tricycle Theatre, UK and international tour); *Dunsinane* (RSC at Hampstead Theatre); *Creditors* (Donmar Warehouse and BAM); *Damascus* and *Miniskirts of Kabul* (Tricycle Theatre); *Brewers Fayre, Outlying Islands* (Traverse Theatre); *The American Pilot* (RSC, Soho & MTC); *Pyrenees* (Paines Plough); *The Cosmonaut's Last Message to the Woman He Once Loved in the Former Soviet Union* (Donmar Warehouse); *The Architect* and *Europe* (Traverse Theatre). Adaptations include: *The Creditors* (Donmar Warehouse and BAM, NYC); *The Bacchae* (Edinburgh International Festival and Lyric Theatre, Hammersmith); *Tintin in Tibet* (Barbican and The Playhouse); *When the Bulbul Stopped Singing* (Traverse Theatre); *Caligula* (Donmar Warehouse); and *Peter Pan* (National Theatre Studio, Traverse/Barbican).

David's work for children and young people includes *The Monster in the Hall* (TAG Theatre Co. Glasgow); *Yellow Moon* (TAG Theatre Co. Glasgow); *Gobbo* (National Theatre of Scotland); *Dr Korczak's Example* (TAG Theatre Co. Glasgow). He has also written extensively for radio.

David is currently under commission to the Almeida Theatre and the National Theatre of Scotland. He is also writing the book of the stage musical *Charlie and the Chocolate Factory* (Warner Bros/Neal St Productions) and an adaptation for the Broadway producer, John Hart.

He is working with Film Four on a screen adaptation of his stage play *Midsummer*. Other films include: *Vinyan* and *A Complicated Kindness*.

Elena Gremina is a playwright and screenwriter. She runs the theatre project Documentary Theatre (TEATR.DOC) and she is a board member and advisor to the Lyubimovka Young Playwrights' Festival. She writes a number of popular and long-running serials for Russian television.

Her plays, which include *Beyond the Looking Glass*, *The Sakhalin Wife* and *Russian Eclipse*, have been staged in many Russian theatres in Moscow, St Petersburg and across the country. She is also the author of several 'verbatim-style' documentary plays: *September.doc* (2005), *1.18* (2010) and *Two in the House* (2011).

She has received a WDR Prize for Best Radioplay (1991), an All-Russian Radioplay Award (1992) and a Stalker Award (2005) for her contribution to Russian theatre.

Sasha Dugdale is a poet and a translator of Russian plays and poetry. Her translations have been produced by the Royal Court, RSC, BBC Radio and in theatres in the US, Ireland and Australia. Her translation of *Plasticine* by Vasily Sigarev is the only foreign-language play to win an ES Best Newcomer Award, and her translations of the poetry of Elena Shvarts, *Birdsong on the Seabed*, were a Poetry Book Society Recommended Translation and shortlisted for the Popescu and Academica Rossica prizes. She has published three collections of poetry. Her most recent collection *Red House* was published in 2011 by Carcanet / OxfordPoets.

OTHER TRICYCLE TITLES

THE GREAT GAME: AFGHANISTAN
Richard Bean, Simon Stephens, David Edgar, David Greig, Stephen Jeffreys, Ron Hutchinson,
Amit Gupta, Joy Wilkinson, Lee Blessing, Colin Teevan, Abi Morgan and Ben Ockrent
9781840029222

BLOODY SUNDAY – SCENES
FROM THE SAVILLE INQUIRY
Richard Norton-Taylor
9781840025682

CALLED TO ACCOUNT
Richard Norton-Taylor & Nicolas Kent
9781840027457

THE COLOUR OF JUSTICE – BASED
ON THE TRANSCRIPTS OF THE
STEPHEN LAWRENCE INQUIRY
Richard Norton-Taylor
9781840021073

GUANTANAMO:
"HONOR BOUND TO DEFEND FREEDOM"
Victoria Brittain & Gillian Slovo
9781840024746

JUSTIFYING WAR – SCENES
FROM THE HUTTON INQUIRY
Richard Norton-Taylor
9781840024173

THE RIOTS
Gillian Slovo
9781849431996

SREBRENICA
Nicolas Kent
9781840026276

TACTICAL QUESTIONING – SCENES
FROM THE BAHA MOUSA INQUIRY
Richard Norton-Taylor
9781849430319

WWW.OBERONBOOKS.COM